Saturday Afternoon Fever

Also by Jeff Stelling and available from Headline

Jeffanory: Stories from Beyond Soccer Saturday

I've Got Mail: The Soccer Saturday Letters

JEFF STELLING

Saturday Afternoon Fever

THE AUTOBIOGRAPHY

HEADLINE

First published in 2024 by
HEADLINE PUBLISHING GROUP

3

Hardback ISBN 978 1 4722 7981 1

Printed and bound in Great Britain by Clays Ltd, Elcograf S.p.A.

Headline's policy is to use papers that are natural, renewable and recyclable
products and made from wood grown in well-managed forests and other
controlled sources. The logging and manufacturing processes are expected
to conform to the environmental regulations of the country of origin.

HEADLINE PUBLISHING GROUP
An Hachette UK Company
Carmelite House
50 Victoria Embankment
London EC4Y 0DZ

www.headline.co.uk
www.hachette.co.uk

To Lizzie, Robbie, Matt, Olivia,

and my constant companion Stan (2012–2023),

without whom my charmed life will

never quite be the same.

Contents

INTRODUCTION

I am sitting in my office in my Hampshire home 300 miles from my native North East. The autumnal sun is streaming through the window blinds, warming my old dogs Stan, Lottie and Meg who are lying at my feet. I am trying to work out how to start on the story of the life of this old dog, almost seventy years now, and my love of football, which has lasted very nearly as long.

On the wall in front of me, my five consecutive Sports Broadcaster of the Year awards are framed alongside a certificate giving me the Freedom of the Borough of Hartlepool. Below them, on a bookcase strewn with paperwork and football reference books, is my Sports Journalists' Association Lifetime Achievement trophy and my Variety Club Heart for Services to Sport. A bronze statuette of Brian Clough given to me by Middlesbrough Borough Council stands tall. My Roath Ravers mug, a gift from the club, is there too, ready for the dishwasher. On the window ledge to my right are my personalised photos from Phil Collins and Gordon Banks. Next to them, in its white wooden frame, a treasured shot of the *Soccer Saturday* team of Matt Le Tissier, Paul Merson, Phil Thompson and Charlie Nicholas. Alongside is a photo of their predecessors George Best, Rodney Marsh, Frank McLintock and Clive Allen.

On the small wooden table behind me are my gleaming silver Television and Radio Industries Club awards for being their Sports Presenter of the Year in 2012, 2016 and 2017, next to a Just Giving Charity Fundraiser of the Year trophy. A crystal inscribed 'I cracked the Crystal Maze' is almost hidden. It should really be inscribed 'A J Pritchard cracked the Crystal Maze – but I was there too'. On the wall at my back is a framed black Prostate Cancer UK t-shirt marking over a million pounds raised for the charity, an American Screen Actors Guild award for 'outstanding performances' in *Ted Lasso* and a caricature of me, arms aloft, in the Hartlepool United football kit.

Looking around and trying to take it all in, I can only scratch my head. How did all this happen to a chubby kid from a working class family on the Rift House Estate? A boy whose passion for football was never going to be matched by his ability to play the game? As someone may have once said, it has frankly been 'Unbelievable Jeff!'

1

THE NIGHT MY SISTER DANCED WITH BRIAN CLOUGH

Brian Clough was a young man himself, just 30, when he took over as manager of League Two Hartlepool United with his faithful sidekick Peter Taylor alongside him.

He arrived from non-league Burton Albion, tasked with dragging the club away from their regular position at or near the foot of the old fourth division. First football league management jobs simply don't get any tougher. On the pitch the club had been forced to apply for re-election just over a year earlier, a far too regular occurrence. Off it, there was no money. A temporary stand erected in 1919 was still standing. There weren't even any floodlights. Clough was not only expected to take charge of the team, he was also expected to help with painting Victoria Park and occasionally driving the team coach. For this he was paid £2,000 a year plus £500 if Pools finished in the top half of the table, something they did in his second season in charge when they ended the campaign in eighth place. It was about as unlikely a feat as Leicester City winning the Premier League in 2016.

But there was an unlikely bonus for young Clough as he got to dance – and have a peck on the cheek – with my lovely big sister Sue.

The towns of West Hartlepool and Hartlepool amalgamated in 1967 and Sue was chosen as the first ever 'Miss Hartlepool'. When she had been in her early teens, with her tied-back hair and round framed glasses, no one would ever have guessed she would turn swan-like into such a beautiful young woman. As part of her duties, she was required to have the first dance at the town's amalgamation ball with Brian. She was just seventeen and a sixth former at the local girls' high school. I'm not sure if he introduced himself with 'Now then young woman', but it wouldn't surprise me. My brothers Tony and Peter were older than me and the three of us shared a bedroom in our new council house in Hartlepool – the boys had burned down the previous one by setting off fireworks inside. They got a rocket from my dad for that!

They were accident prone. Peter broke his arm falling out of a tree. Tony's accident was significantly more spectacular. He fell 85 feet down a lift shaft on to a concrete floor on his first foreign holiday in Spain, mistaking it for the entrance to the toilet. It was an old fashioned style lift with a grill across the front, opening in theory on to the lift floor. But not on this occasion. The lift was at the top of the shaft. Instead my brother stepped into thin air. Not only was it a miracle he survived the fall but also that no one had used the lift in the immediate aftermath before the alarm was raised as he would surely have been crushed to death. He was flown home like a mummy after breaking pretty much every bone in his body. My dad was blue lighted to Manchester airport to meet his flight as he was stretchered off the plane. Tony was off work for more than a year and doctors told us that if he hadn't had a *cerveza* or two (or ten), relaxing his body, he would almost certainly have been killed.

I was closest to Sue, partly I suppose due to the smaller age gap. She was five years older than me. We would walk to school together, her in her pork pie hat, me in my maroon blazer – the boys' grammar school was on the way to the girls' high school – and I would nag her relentlessly to take me to see Pools play. In those days, the football environment was very working class, very adult and very male. My mum and dad were reluctant to let me go alone so unless Sue would take me, I was limited to dashing in when the gates of the ramshackle ground opened ten minutes from time, just as the great majority of people were coming out after another defeat. Sue was no lover of football and no lover of the atmosphere, but from time to time she would relent and be my chaperone. I didn't notice at the time that she would be the only woman – well girl, actually – in the entire crowd and that the language was bad enough to make a grown man's ears burn let alone a teenage girl. Though my dad was used to industrial language at work, it was totally banned in the Stelling household, so my sister probably learned quite a bit of new vocabulary.

But I was in love with it and couldn't get enough. I remember Sue and I were in a crowd of more than 7,000 to see Pools beat Workington 3–1 in the first round of the FA Cup. I am pretty sure Willie McPheat scored twice. I am pretty sure too he never scored for Pools before or after that! We went on to reach the third round that season and I was heartbroken when we lost 3–1 at top of the old first division Huddersfield Town to two late goals. I still remember the back page of the *Daily Express* with the headline: 'Only 5 minutes more Hartlepool!'

Sue had been seeing a local boy, Colin, for quite some time and after she left school and university, they were engaged to be married. He was a local fishmonger's son – make up your own jokes – who was in the navy and away at sea for months at a time. It wasn't an ideal scenario for a relationship. It was Colin who first disillusioned me that I was a healthy fish-eater. A nutritious portion of tripe and onions was often on the dinner table at my home in Catcote Road. I was convinced that shoals of tripe swam below the surface of the North Sea. After all it looked like fish, even if it didn't taste like it. When he told me, with his family expertise, that it had never been anywhere near the briny but was the lining of a cow's or pig's stomach, I am afraid it was off the menu.

My sister was by now a qualified accountant and was spending more and more time with one of her work colleagues. The inevitable happened – the engagement was off. Her new boyfriend, Tony Harbron, was an incredibly introverted character, who refused to meet our family for months and when he did was so shy, he barely spoke. I was working at the local radio station, Radio Tees, when I discovered Tony's mum had also been working there as a cleaner for months. Her son had apparently told her not to approach me at the studios. Perhaps he was embarrassed that she should be doing a job he felt was menial. But he shouldn't have been. My mum had been a nurse, but with times hard, she was now working as a cleaner herself at the nearby comprehensive school.

So their eventual wedding was a slightly strange affair, with the Stelling side of the aisle packed but just Tony's mum and younger brother on the other side. Eventually they moved for work to Burton on Trent. We tried to stay in touch. When I married, we went to London for our honeymoon. Believe me, daft as it might sound now, that was the height of adventure for a Hartlepool lad. I had only been to the capital once before, when I was at junior school. We went to see *Oliver Twist* on a school trip and watched the recording of ITV's *Five O'Clock Club*. I was a bit disappointed that the star act was a bloke I had never heard of, with an unusual voice who sang in dark glasses. What I would have given to see Roy Orbison twenty years later.

By chance Sue and Tony were there at the same time we were on our honeymoon and came and had dinner with us at the Cumberland Hotel in Oxford Street. But there was no doubt she was slipping away, or being drawn away, from me and my family.

The truth is I almost saw more of Brian Clough. He went into management after his brilliant playing career had been ended prematurely. He was bright, brash, a little eccentric, an individual thinker with an eye for great PR – he was pictured driving the Hartlepool United team bus to highlight how short of money we were, though I suspect it was only until he was out of camera shot. But he was already a great motivator with a brilliant if unorthodox football brain. People rarely talked about him in the singular. It was always 'Clough and Taylor'. They were every bit as much of a double act as Peter Cook and Dudley Moore or Eric Morecambe and Ernie Wise. It was hard to imagine one without the other by his side. Taylor was often seen as the yin to Clough's yang. I viewed him as a type of brake, someone to slow down Brian sufficiently to allow pause for thought. Whatever the chemistry, it worked from the start.

Though the team didn't win promotion, the football world could see something special in Clough. When Derby County came calling, an offer of £3,250 a year was not enough to make him stay at Hartlepool. He naturally took Peter Taylor with him. His successes there and at Nottingham Forest make him, in my mind, one of the greatest football managers of my lifetime. No one at Hartlepool ever forgot what he did for the club. And he never forgot the chance it gave him. Soon after joining Derby he paid £6,000 to Pools for a spindly young Scottish teenager called John McGovern. And when yet another financial crisis threatened to engulf Hartlepool, Clough paid inflated fees for two more players, Tony Parry and John Sheridan, principally to help his old club. There would be a continuing bond between the two clubs. Many years after Clough had moved on, they met in the FA Cup third round. After the game, County donated their share of the takings to Hartlepool.

I remember at the height of his fame being sent to interview Clough after his all-conquering Forest side had played Middlesbrough at Ayresome Park. The plan was to doorstep him as he left. And I did. As he walked to his car I approached him and once inside, he wound down his window and I did the interview through the open car window – a bit different from these days when every inter-view has to take place in a sanitised room under the beady eye of a press officer and in front of the assembled media. The days of exclusives have disappeared. Unfortunately, so did my interview with Clough. I had unforgivably forgotten to put any tape in my old reel-to-reel recorder.

Later, when Radio Tees decided to hold a charity fund-raising day, as sports editor I was tasked with the job of approaching every top division side for items to auction. Aside from Boro, not one replied to my letters (e-mail didn't exist of course). Then one lunchtime, the newsroom secre-tary told me she had Brian Clough on the line. I thought she was kidding. Clough was by now famous as one of the most successful managers in world football and infamous as being one of the most difficult and controversial. But it was no joke. Clough asked me what the station wanted and within seconds had agreed to send a host of shirts and footballs from the European champions.

Football though was a very different beast in those days. I remember when Graeme Souness left Middlesbrough to join Liverpool. I had spoken to Graeme of course while covering Boro, but didn't know him particularly well. When the story broke I left messages for him, but couldn't track him down. I was working late that evening when the phone in the office rang. It was Graeme returning my call and happy to be interviewed. Imagine that happening in this day and age! This was a huge transfer. Liverpool had just signed Kenny Dalglish and Alan Hansen. It was a pivotal day in the life of Souness and yet he had taken the time to ring back a cub reporter. Many years later when I hosted the Champions League show, he would introduce me to other world-famous ex-pros as one of his oldest friends. He had the good grace not to mention that we hadn't seen or spoken to each other at all for about thirty years.

Of course it was no surprise he was a huge success at Anfield. But, on his return to the North East with his new club, he and I were both brought crashing to earth. The entire Liverpool squad was at the official opening of Willie Maddren's sports shop in Stockton-on-Tees high street when the floor gave way beneath our feet sending millions of pounds worth of footballers and yours truly tumbling into the cellar below. Willie reckoned it was my weight that did it. Amid the broken floorboards, falling plaster and clouds of dust, I had the presence of mind to set my tape recorder on to record as we crashed through the floor – this time it did have tape in it! Thankfully, the fall had been no more than

10 feet or so and no one was hurt – and this time I really did have an exclusive.

*

In 1981, I moved to London where Sue was to become quite literally a sight for sore eyes.

I had taken a job at the London based station LBC/IRN. Like most journalists in those days the dream was to work in Fleet Street and this was as near as you could get – in Gough Square around 20 yards from the hub of the British newspaper industry. Walking down that street past the offices of the *Daily Telegraph* and the *Daily Express*, the Reuters Agency and so many others gave me a real buzz. Day and night it was busy with newspaper, radio and agency reporters, printers and compositors, and delivery drivers waiting to get papers onto the streets as soon as they came hot off the press. Almost as good, it was next door to the world famous Ye Olde Cheshire Cheese pub with its sawdust spread across its wooden floors. Wherever there are journalists there are pubs and I would spend time in most of them. The Punch Tavern, the Cock, the Mitre, El Vino . . . the choice was almost endless. My wife and I moved into a rented one-bedroom ground floor flat on the scruffy, litter strewn North End Road, close to the market where Esther Rantzen used to do interviews for the rating-topping consumer show *That's Life*. It had a shared kitchen, a tin shower in the corner of the bedroom, a TV that ran on fifty pence pieces, a punk rock band in the flat above and overlooked a burger bar. Yes, we were really living the high life! At least *we* had the only key for the downstairs toilet.

The job should have been great. I often presented their flagship Saturday afternoon show *Sportswatch*, but if not I would be at a London match. The station made me its athletics correspondent, a role which would see me travel to the likes of Brisbane, Athens, Zagreb, Helsinki and eventually the Los Angeles Olympics. But the truth was that, initially at least, I didn't enjoy it.

Soon after I started I developed a bad eye infection. I wore contact lenses, or at least tried to. In those days the lenses were nothing like these days, malleable, featherlight and tiny. They were the size of soup bowls and every morning I would have a running battle to force them into my eyes. When I woke one day to find my right eye bright red and oozing an unpleasant substance, I called my optician straightaway. She packed me off to the Western Eye Hospital on Marylebone Road where after a long wait a totally disinterested doctor gave me some drops, an eye patch and told me to come back in 48 hours. If I had listened, I would have lost my eye and my future would have been very different.

Instead the following day, now unable to open the eye at all, I headed for Moorfields Eye Hospital. It was like an Indian railway station at rush hour. I had never seen so many people. I took my place at the back of a thirty-strong queue just to put my name down to be seen. As I stood in line, a nurse passed me. She stopped in her tracks. 'Oh, my goodness,' she said and immediately took me aside. Within minutes I was being seen by a doctor, who insisted on the immediate use of a powerful antibiotic. The quickest way to administer this was by injection – into the eyeball. It was the most horrifying thing that had ever happened to me. Three nurses held me down, one gripping each arm tightly against the sides of the chair in which I was sitting, another holding my head, as the doctor injected my eyeball. I would have loved to have closed my eyes to avoid seeing the size of the needle. It was the first and only time in my life that my knees have ever knocked uncontrollably. When it was over the nurses told me many people faint – I am not surprised.

Within half an hour I was in a hospital bed. I called my wife and asked her to bring pyjamas – she had to go and buy some as I didn't own any – and a toothbrush. When the consultant first visited me he told me he could not guarantee how much sight I would retain in my eye. He also told me had I waited a further 48 hours, I would have been blind in my right eye. Throughout the first couple of days, nurses put drops in my eye every 15 minutes, including throughout the night. My mood was low. I was surrounded by mainly elderly people who were blind or partially sighted with no idea of what would happen to me.

My wife spent as much time as she could with me but had to work. I had been in London for such a short time that I hadn't developed any strong friendships. When I told work I needed some time off, I suspect they thought I was skiving. My parents lived in the North East, so I was basically on my own.

It was on the fourth day that through my one good eye, I saw a figure approaching my bedside unannounced. It was Sue. It was so uplifting. I have no idea what we talked about but a week later she was back. The truth is I felt closer than ever to her.

Things were looking up too with the prognosis of my eye. It was badly scarred where the infection had burrowed its way in, but doctors now believed that I would keep a minimum of 50 per cent of my vision. In a more positive mood, I realised what an astonishing place Moorfields is. Not only would they save my eye, but almost every day someone would have bandages removed after an operation on a detached retina or cataract. The joy of others regaining sight is infectious.

I was anxious to return home and day after day badgered the nurses and doctors, but it was always one more day. Towards the end of the second week, I was told I could have an hour out of bed and out of the ward. I had a plan. One of my favourite nurses conspiratorially guided me out of the hospital – not that I needed it as my sight was rapidly returning – and to the threshold of paradise. The pub next door. In my dressing gown and new pyjamas, I pushed open the door to discover a thriving clutch of drinkers, almost all of them in dressing gowns and pyjamas! I half expected to see Jack Nicholson out of *One Flew Over the Cuckoo's Nest*.

After a fortnight, I was discharged. My sight loss eventually was estimated at 5 to 10 per cent, though even now opticians always take a step back when they see the scar tissue during eyesight tests. Moorfields, one of the world's great medical institutions, had saved my sight. And just as surely my sister Sue had helped save my sanity.

•

I got the call that Sue was dead one Friday morning. She had woken feeling unwell and gone to her kitchen for water. She collapsed and never recovered consciousness. She was thirty-four. A coroner's inquest revealed Sue had died of acute liver failure.

By now I was working at TV-am in Camden Town. It was my first television job. I had been on screen a number of times presenting sports bulletins – the legendary David Frost introduced my first ever on-screen appearance. But I had never presented the channel's early morning Saturday sports programme. When I say early morning, it really was: a 90-minute collection of sports features and interviews that was on air at 6 a.m. You can imagine how many viewers it got! But it would be my first real TV breakthrough. I was due to front the show the day after my sister had died. I talked it through with my wife and we decided, I would do the show and travel back to the North East to join my grieving family immediately afterwards. So I told no one at TV-am what had happened, prepped all day Friday and hosted the programme on Saturday. I even think I stayed for breakfast afterwards. God knows what I was thinking of. It is a decision I am ashamed of to this day and I will be until the day I die. To put ambition before my family was unforgiveable.

Sue's husband Tony was, of course, at the funeral, but I never saw him again after that. My dad, Andy, a tough ex-steelworker, shrank into himself. He had always been popular in town, so much so that a shopping trip with him was a nightmare. Everyone knew Andy and wanted to talk to him. But now he had little to say. He had always been a big man but he began to fade away. Not long afterwards, my dad suffered a burst aorta. I was by his bedside but there was nothing that could be done. He had died quite literally of a broken heart.

2

THE STAR LETTER

In 1976, Alf Wood joined Middlesbrough after successful spells at Shrewsbury and Millwall and a less productive period at Hull City.

Shortly afterwards, I joined the local station Radio Tees after a successful four-year spell at the *Hartlepool Mail*. At least I thought it was successful, but then again I had joined the paper partly because I had clear proof in black and white (well black and green actually) that I would make a decent journalist! The proof turned out to be less convincing than I had first imagined.

I had been one of the top students at my junior school at Rift House, which was just two minutes from our home, a red breeze block semi-detached house on a main road through the town. It hadn't been a main road when we had first moved in. It was a cul-de-sac leading directly on to open countryside, almost idyllic, until the bulldozers moved in. Though it was a council estate, it had a lovely feel to it. I can still remember now that Mrs Young was the neighbour on our right and Mrs Dawson on the left. Everyone knew everyone. No one locked their doors. Visitors would just turn up, tap on the door and let themselves in. As I had aunts, uncles and cousins living within 100 yards, there was a regular stream of visitors – though you didn't have to be related to come calling. With few households having telephones, every visit in those days was impromptu. In the early 80s we were offered the chance to buy the house, but my dad chose not to. It wasn't the price that put him off, more the fact that the 'Right to Buy' policy had come from Margaret Thatcher and dad was convinced nothing that came from 'The Devil Woman' as he called her could possibly be beneficial.

The transition to senior school was tougher than I imagined. In truth, I hadn't really wanted to pass my eleven-plus as, at Hartlepool Grammar School, they played rugby not football. No football was impossible to contemplate. It was a huge part of my life, not just watching and playing. My friends and I would collect and compare football stickers. We bought football comics, *Roy of the Rovers* and *Scorcher*, whenever we could afford them. We organised a Subbuteo League with set fixture lists and kick-off times played in homes all across the town.

Being fat didn't help either. I had escaped much teasing at my previous school but now was starting afresh. I hated PE lessons in particular as I cut a less than impressive figure in shorts and vest and couldn't do so much as a forward roll or a handstand. I couldn't impress others by showing I was a half decent footballer despite my build. It was a difficult time. I remember one day going into the very grand red brick buildings of the school wearing my new made-to measure brown corduroy jacket. None of my clothes could be off the peg as nothing fitted me, so my parents at huge personal cost would have things individually made. At the first break of the day, I got into a confrontation with another boy who slashed the sleeve of my jacket with his metal comb. A swathe of material was hanging loose. I did not know how to explain this to my mum and dad who had worked so many hours to pay for my now badly damaged jacket.

Gradually I did develop a group of friends though, principally those who shared my passion for football. Many years later I would get a call about one of the boys who had helped me through the tough times, who had been a member of the Subbuteo League and who had been one of my closest friends. Roger Thurston was an easy going and very good-hearted boy, one of the most popular in the school. He was much better at Subbuteo than I was and much more academic. He went on to be an optician with his own practice in the town. The call was to tell me Roger had hung himself.

I wasn't much good at anything at school. My reports were littered with 'poor, fair, must try harder' comments. I was actually trying bloody hard, but I just wasn't very bright. My term-time performance was always much better than my exam grades, in part because I had my brilliant sister's help to fall back on for homework and in part because my best mate John Hunt let me copy his stuff in class. But I did get good English marks and my essay writing was ok and I had a vague idea that I might become a journalist. The school headmaster, an intimidating, black-robed, cane-wielding, almost Dickensian character, so thin his skin was almost translucent, was unimpressed. I was beckoned to his study – never, ever a good sign.

'Stelling, no boy from this school will ever do something as disreputable as being a journalist!' He almost spat the words out. In those days, many towns had a 'green 'un' or a 'pink 'un', a football version of the local newspaper which was published soon after Saturday's matches had finished. In days before the internet it was the fans' bible – the only way to get results, tables and match reports. The *Football Mail* in Hartlepool hit the streets every Saturday at about 5.30. As well as a report on that day's big game and some local league football reports, there was a letters page. The 'Star Letter' each week won a £10 prize. As a boy from a council estate, this was big money to me, so I decided to try my luck. I wrote to the newspaper. The following week I opened its green and black pages and there it was. My letter was the 'Star Letter'! I had earned £10. A fortnight later I wrote again with the same outcome. My letter was the 'Star Letter'. And so it went on. My letters to the *Football Mail* became a regular source of income. If I'd had any doubts about my future career, now I had none. I had proved I could write. I would be a journalist. It was only when I got my first job in journalism at the *Hartlepool Mail* that I discovered the truth. I introduced myself to the sports editor, Arthur Pickering, as blunt a man as you will ever meet, and grandly announced that I was the author of all those fine 'Star Letters'. He brought me down to earth with a resounding bump.

'They weren't just the Star Letters pal,' he said, 'they were the only fucking letters. We had to make the rest up ourselves to fill the page.' It wasn't something the Leveson Inquiry would have been too bothered about, but I felt I had become a journalist by default.

•

Alf Wood was a striker who was less than prolific at Boro – he only ever scored two goals for them – and wasn't in the twelve who would be involved at Anfield against Liverpool one Saturday near the end of his time at the club. But he was expected to be there. He asked me how I would be getting to the game. I usually travelled in the (not so) trusty green company Hillman Imp. Alf offered me a lift if I would share the petrol money. So we did. He picked me up in a layby off the A19. When we got to the ground, he headed for the dressing rooms and I headed for the press box.

It's unlikely these days that Reece James would drive himself to a Chelsea away match if he wasn't starting and offer an LBC reporter a lift for a share of the petrol. Or Jamie Vardy would offer to pick up the Leicester local radio commentator on the A50. It made me think just how much has changed in my lifetime on the fringes of the game.

Welshman John Neal was manager of Middlesbrough at the time. He was quiet and considered with a slightly monotone voice – not exactly great interview material – but he was unfailingly obliging and polite.

He would take the Boro squad to Aberystwyth to run them fit pre-season over the giant sand dunes and one year asked me to come. So I drove down to Wales in a rented green Hillman Avenger – the Imp was being used elsewhere, thank god – with Meatloaf's 'Bat Out of Hell' blasting from the cassette player to join them. The first thing I saw when I arrived at the university campus where the squad was staying, was Tony McAndrew, one of the team's hard men throwing up into a bucket by the side of his bed. I soon found out why. The sand dunes there are like the foothills of the Himalayas. The players had been doing shuttles up and down them. I tried the following day and managed a couple. I also soon discovered the benefit of having a bucket by the bed.

This was a decent Boro team, mid-table in the top flight with the likes of David Armstrong, Tony McAndrew, David Mills, Stan Cummins, Stuart Boam and Graeme Souness – and I was living with them in their Spartan student accommodation, training with them and drinking with them. There was not a press officer in sight, no one to vet who said what about who. It was a relationship based on trust, something that has sadly disappeared over the years. Again it is a scenario that could not happen in this day and age.

Nowadays pretty much all interviews with clubs at most professional levels are orchestrated. At the start of each week the Premier League sends out a list of eight or ten players who will be available for interview. Of course they are never, or hardly ever, the ones you really want. They usually don't really want to do it either. And every media outlet gets the same access. The days of nurturing contacts and getting a scoop are gone. I've almost stopped reading Saturday's newspapers because the stories are all the same. It is no fault of the journalists. They're in an editorial straight-jacket.

It is the same with those managerial press conferences, man managed so that no one can ask a half decent question, and if one does slip through the net, the press officer jumps in before it can be answered. In those Middlesbrough days I could interview John Neal alone, at length, and it was up to me as a journalist to try and ask the right questions to get a story. It was the same with Jack Charlton, his predecessor, albeit he wouldn't say a word before I had given him a nice crisp £5 note for his trouble. I tell you, that was good value! I remember on one run along the beach during that pre-season camp, Willie Maddren, a fine player who was an England Under-23 international and must have been close to full honours at times, was battling his way back from a serious injury. Willie never got back to the player he was and told me the day he knew he was finished was when I overtook him during a run along the beach! Poor Willie, a lovely footballer and a lovely man, suffered from motor neurone disease and died far too young at forty-nine.

On my returns to the North East these days I still see the playing field where the local kids from the Rift House estate would play matches every single day. The field is still there but you don't see kids play there anymore, which is a concern. Of course there is a lot more organised football for them, but I think it's a shame those impromptu FA Cup/ World Cup finals with your mates are not a part of growing up any more.

The local 'rec' is still there too at Rift House. It is where I played my Sunday morning football, though I saw a couple of years ago the council was charging over £400 per club to play there. And I thought we were encouraging people to stay fit not fat. There's no better way than playing football.

Our team used to split our pre-season training between there and the local beach at Seaton Carew. One season we started too early in the year and turned up to find no goalposts. 'Just imagine the goalposts,' said our legendary manager Dennis. I have never scored so many in a single game. Once a week we were on the beach, running over sand dunes – thankfully smaller than those in Wales. Training used to have to stop on the dot at 8.30 though to give us time to get to our local pub, the Traveller's Rest, to have a skinful before closing time.

The standard in the Sunday League was ridiculously high. Most weeks, players who had turned out for Hartlepool United would play for one of the better Sunday League teams too, to supplement their income. And the big games could get a couple of hundred people watching.

We weren't one of the better teams and didn't get so many watching, which was just as well the day I got my marching orders after a running battle with a tricky little winger called Brian Doughty. I was a full-back and spent most of the game kicking him in the air. He was mouthy and spent most of the game giving me a lot of stick. It ended in a fist fight that provoked a twenty-two-man brawl and sending-offs for both of us (red cards had not been invented then). Brian actually turned out to be a really good bloke and ended up marrying my cousin Gill. He also went on to be a referee – talk about poacher turned gamekeeper!

We used to get changed in our cars or in pokey, unlit, unheated dressing rooms with toilets that were filthy and didn't flush. I know from coaching one of my son's teams at under-16 and under-17 level that often this is still the case. Even in affluent Winchester, the changing facilities were shocking with no showers and filthy toilets that nobody in their right mind would ever use. With the game at the higher level awash with money, it is disgraceful that this is still allowed to be the case.

At many levels though, the game, and everything that surrounds it, has changed, mostly, but by no means always, for the better. Let's not kid ourselves, virtually all of this, good, bad and indifferent, is down to TV money. Without the rights' fees TV pays, there would be no big money owners, no new stadia or facilities, no multi-million pound players.

The actual coverage itself has been one of the biggest differences. If you weren't at a game on Saturday there was no real way of keeping up with how your team was doing.

Getting to away games was pretty much impossible. Train services were awful, most motorways had not been built – the M25 wasn't even a twinkle in Mrs Thatcher's eye – cars were slower and less reliable and besides, we didn't own one. My dad did once buy a motorbike from a friend at work but it stood untouched in our garden, never ridden. If Pools were playing away, the first we would know about the outcome was when we huddled round our open fire, burning fingers as we toasted bread that was perched on the end of a two-pronged fork while waiting for Frank Bough on *Grandstand* to announce it was time for the teleprinter which, painfully slowly, would spit out Halifax 1 Hartlepool 0 or something similar.

The arrival of teletext, daft as it seems now, revolution-ised Saturdays as we crowded around our TV to watch the football text pages slowly click round, one by one through each division, pausing for perhaps 30 seconds on each set of scores. It always seemed to take an eternity to get to my team's latest score and when it did get there you usually wished it hadn't.

As for live football, when I was a kid the only game you could watch as it happened was the FA Cup final. Otherwise it was half an hour's black and white highlights on a Sunday afternoon. In the North East this was a programme called *Shoot* on Tyne Tees TV presented by a man called George Taylor, who looked like he worked in the local branch of Barclays Bank for the rest of the week and may well have done so for all I know. It usually consisted of 20 minutes of

Newcastle United's game, if they were at home (Tyne Tees was based in Newcastle so it was much more convenient) plus a couple of minutes of Sunderland and Middlesbrough and a minute or so each of Hartlepool and Darlington.

Nowadays of course it is impossible to avoid football on the TV – just ask my wife! Every angle on and off the pitch is covered by a multitude of cameras, there are slow motion replays, freeze frames, every gadget possible for the army of pundits to illustrate their point pre-match, post-match, mid-match, on highlights shows. Is it better for it? Of course it is – a million per cent better. But can there be too much televised football? During the Covid-19 pandemic when every Premier League match was covered live – rightly so with fans not allowed at the grounds – I have to admit it got to the stage where I could barely watch. As part of my job I felt duty bound to wade through every game no matter how good, bad or insignificant it was. It became hard to be enthusiastic about Crystal Palace against Sheffield United, probably even for fans of Palace and United. Like Tony's Chocolonely caramel sea salt milk chocolate, you can have too much of a good thing.

I know a lot of people enjoyed seeing live football at 3 p.m. on a Saturday but it was important for the good of football in general, when things returned to something like normal after the pandemic, that Premier League games were no longer allowed to be shown live at 3 p.m. on Saturday afternoons. At the moment, they can only be seen in the UK via illegal streams – which I know none of you ever watch!

This has been the case since Bob Lord, then Burnley chairman, came up with the idea to help safeguard clubs sixty-odd years ago. To let matches be televised could kill off lower league clubs. How many people would drag themselves away from the telly or out of the pub on a cold, wet, windy day to watch Colchester United against Barrow if there was live Premier League football on at the time? Even Crystal Palace against Sheffield United might be more appealing. Just order another pint of anaesthetic before it kicks-off.

The argument that this should change was dragged out once again when Cristiano Ronaldo made his second debut for Manchester United in September 2020. Neither Sky nor BT had chosen it as their live game. So when it kicked off at 3 p.m. that Saturday the only places you could follow it live were on BBC Radio 5 Live or better still on *Soccer Saturday* where Paul Merson's vivid description made you think you were at Old Trafford anyway. Every year the arguments over the 3 p.m. blackout continue. One day I am sure it will be lifted, but even if I am old-fashioned in this view, I think that will benefit the few, not the many. If you want to watch football live on Saturday afternoons at 3 p.m., just go to a game.

Of course, facilities are so much better too. I'm willing to argue the point with Roy Keane about the prawn sandwich brigade. I quite like being one of them – though no prawns please. They are bad for my gout. But it is nice being able to have a decent meal and drink before a game and I'm sorry, but I prefer sitting to standing. When I was a teenager I used to go to St James' Park from time to time if Pools were not playing. I would stand among the thousands packed into the Gallowgate end and like waves, sway forwards and backwards with the crowd as required. It was impossible not to. It wasn't so much the potential danger of the situation that put me off, more the warm drizzle you would feel down the back of your leg from time to time as the fan behind you, unable to extricate himself from the sardine-packed crowd, had to find some outlet for the four pints of Exhibition he had drunk before the game. Also, being slightly vertically challenged – 5 feet 7 and a quarter, above average height for a man . . . in Guatemala – you really only saw half the game, mainly the dull bits. My oldest son Rob, also a Pools fan (brought up right) still prefers standing at grounds where he can. But he got his genes from his mum and is significantly taller than me. And there aren't so many heads to see over when you are away at Boreham Wood.

Not every ground has Delia Smith-standard food, of course. In fact, when Hartlepool were facing the threat of administration, or worse, liquidation a few seasons ago, even the chip stall was closed down. Apparently frying chips is not cost effective due to the amount of electricity it uses. So, if you suddenly find your club has closed its chippie, you should be worried.

The new or modernised stadia these days don't just boast restaurants and bars but toilets where you don't expect to get dysentery after every visit, and have encouraged families to come to matches together, improving the atmosphere and the language used significantly. My sister Sue would have felt much more at home (though obviously not at South-ampton against Portsmouth).

•

As new fans have been introduced to the game I have loved all my life, I worry that the disconnect between the clubs and their supporters has become greater. Nothing illustrated that better than the plans for a European Super League backed by six of England's biggest and oldest clubs. The money-grabbing, asset-protecting owners tried to treat their fans like serfs, imposing their view on them like Lords of the Manor. They underestimated the power of the football fan, thank goodness.

It showed that supporters do feel a connection with their clubs and their players even though most these days will never get to meet the stars that they pay hard-earned cash to watch week-in, week-out. Clubs like Manchester United, for example, have a back route out of Old Trafford so their players don't have to face the fans. Their training ground at Carrington is so well protected that fans wait at a set of traffic lights half a mile down the road. If the lights are on red, they might get a glimpse of one of United's super-stars before their Bentley pulls away. The images of Arsenal players seeming to ignore a young mascot before their game against West Ham in 2023 and Leeds United stars failing to acknowledge a young fan before a game at Bournemouth were unpalatable. I know that in both cases the dads of the mascots defended the players, saying they had interacted with their sons, but it was still a very bad look for the two clubs.

I am not sure how we got to this stage. In the 60s and 70s, United's neighbours City used to stage a pantomime for the supporters every Christmas. I remember giant goalkeeper Joe Corrigan told me he played Widow Twankey. After away games the players would go back to Maine Road and have a drink at the supporters' club. These were superstar players of their day too – Mike Summerbee, Franny Lee, Colin Bell. I know some players even in this day and age would enjoy more interaction with fans but sadly, it seems, those days are gone. I was so disappointed that the Lionesses slipped out of a private exit at Heathrow after finishing runners-up in the 2023 World Cup. I know it was 6.20 a.m. and I know they had been on a 24-hour flight, but young fans were waiting for them in Terminal 3. Afterwards Georgia Stanway explained this was an FA decision. I don't doubt her word, but surely someone could have had the nous to insist that the players should come out of the main exit. They must have been aware that a reception committee was likely after they had narrowly failed to come back with the World Cup. This was an own goal of significant proportions, especially as so many column inches had been used to explain that the team was inspiring the next generation. Sadly, social media accounts usually run by companies or individuals employed by the player are as close as most fans get to interaction.

Thank goodness every so often someone like Jack Grealish comes along and shows that it is possible to behave like a normal person rather than a protected member of the rarified, superstar footballer species. He is a breath of fresh air (well, more likely a breath of stale booze-tainted air if it is during his summer holidays). My boy Matt bumped into him in a London bar one night and said Jack was brilliant with him. He is though, an easy target. I remember being at a Solihull Moors game one evening, just a couple of corner-kicks away from Jack's old stomping ground at Villa Park. Rather than concentrate on the game, a fan in front of me kept mouthing off about Grealish, complaining about his drinking and diving, that he was out of control, that he would never make it at Manchester City. Even his dad is worried about him, he announced. On and on went this tirade until finally a man standing next to me tapped him on the shoulder.

'How well do you know Jack's dad?' he asked. 'He's a mate,' came the reply. My neighbour waited a few seconds before saying quietly but firmly 'I am Jack's dad.' The loud-mouth critic was silenced and, surprise, surprise, failed to appear again after half-time. And Jack has proven him emphatically wrong about his time at City. The more relatable characters that we have in the game like Jack Grealish, James Maddison and Declan Rice the better in my opinion. And not in that way – Declan doesn't drink!

3

KAMMY

At around the same time that Alf Wood was signing on at Ayresome Park, another Boro boy was making his professional football debut.

We had been born two years and eight miles apart on either side of the River Tees, yet grew up blissfully unaware of how big an impact we would have on each other's lives in years to come. His name was Chris Kamara.

It was no surprise we had not met. In those days it required two buses, the second of them very infrequent, to travel from Hartlepool to Port Clarence, the exotically named but desperately neglected collection of houses that marked the terminus on the north side of the river for the Transporter Bridge that linked the two towns. The Transporter is a bridge that you neither drive nor walk over. Instead you stand or park on the platform which then carries people and cars to the opposite bank. Not surprisingly there are thought to be only two of them still operational worldwide. The Transporter Bridge is a brilliant engineering feat – but impractical and slow. With a bus needed on the other side too to get to central Middlesbrough, the trip could take up to two hours. I could have got to the south bank of the Thames almost as quickly as the south bank of the Tees. It was a journey few people made in either direction.

Kammy had been bought out of the Royal Navy for the sum of £200 by Portsmouth football club at the start of a journey which would take him to Swindon, Brentford, Stoke, Leeds, Luton, Sheffield United and Bradford City. He would revisit Bradford and Stoke as a manager.

He was a good player, no question. Anyone who plays professional football is a good player. And anyone who makes over 640 appearances and scores seventy-one goals is a very good player. But it wasn't a career that would ever bring him nationwide recognition and adoration. It wasn't until he appeared on Sky Sports that he became a household name.

By then I had established myself as the presenter of *Soccer Saturday*. I always describe it as a football show with a difference in that you see no football – no shots, no near misses and no goals – just a panel telling you what you are missing. So I suppose I shouldn't have been too surprised when the show's producer, Ian Condron, decided it might be a good idea to send a reporter to a game, facing the camera and therefore having his back to the action throughout the 90 minutes! The first reporter to do this on British TV was Chris Kamara. We dubbed it Kammy-cam and he single-handedly paved the way for hundreds of reporters who would make careers from doing 'in-vision' pieces from live games.

In my view the success hinged on Kammy's warmth and humour, his ability to misidentify a goal scorer in a flash and his inability to pronounce Papa Bouba Diop, no matter how many times he tried. But he also had an in-depth knowledge of football. People loved him. He had a regular slot on *Soccer AM*, giving viewers guided tours of the inner sanctums of stadiums. He would mischievously swap shirts of starting players with those of the subs – the rub-a-dubs as he called them. Or burst into Harry Redknapp's office as he and assistant Jim Smith were studying the racing in that day's *Sporting Life*.

He was given his own show *Goals on Sunday* which he ran pretty much single-handedly. Kammy would book the guests, who were often a cut above guests on other shows as they were doing it as a personal favour to him. People within the game have huge respect for him and his knowledge. He would decide on topics to discuss and decide which analysis was needed. He would never watch *Match of the Day* on Saturday night as he didn't want his analysis to be influenced by what he had seen and heard on the BBC's flagship football show.

His star was in the ascendency. He was recruited by terrestrial TV to host *Ninja Warrior UK* and later *Cash in the Attic*. He appeared on every celebrity show possible from *Bake Off* to *Through the Keyhole*. He had cameos on *Emmerdale* and *Ted Lasso*. He appeared on stage with the

Kaiser Chiefs and made his own Christmas album. 'Here's to Christmas' reached Number 8 in the UK album charts. His rise and rise was unstoppable – or so it seemed.

On *Soccer Saturday* he endeared himself to the viewers with his unintentional humour. 'It is end to end stuff Jeff, but all at the Forest end', 'Tense and nervous are not the words, though they are the words', 'The atmosphere here is thick and fast' and 'City are fighting like . . . like beavers'. Unintentionally he would introduce the phrase that became part of both of our lives. Kammy didn't realise how often he would start a report with the words 'Unbelievable Jeff!' until we showed him. During one of the *Soccer Saturday* funnies compilations, an assistant producer had edited together around twenty examples of his using the same two words during different reports.

His failure to spot the red card for Anthony Vanden Borre at Portsmouth went viral and to this day is still replayed. By now he and I had become firm friends. We went to the World Cup in Japan where Kammy serenaded anyone who would listen to his version of 'Brown Eyed Girl' as we visited what seemed to be every karaoke bar in the country. We went to the European Championships in Ukraine and watched England beat Sweden with Noel Gallagher, who would have made a great football pundit had he not been a rock megastar. We played golf in Tenerife, though after a night out with Kammy I could not see the ball the next day, let alone hit it. We toured the Midlands as competitors in *Antiques Road Trip* with Roo Irvine and Angus

Ashworth. Chris managed to break a vintage Aston Martin within the first couple of hours. As we were on our way to the first antiques emporium, he fiddled almost subconsciously with the rounded knob at the top of the gear stick until it became detached. Little did he or I know this was not just a decorative feature but an integral part of the gear box. The beautiful electric blue Aston was stuck in gear in the middle of the Leicestershire countryside. With the irate owner on his way to the scene, we decided to make ourselves scarce by thumbing a lift. Cars came past sporadically but in almost 100 per cent of cases the drivers would shout 'Unbelievable Jeff!' And in absolutely 100 per cent of cases, no one stopped! So much for our popularity.

Whoever makes the most profit at auction on their chosen antiques is declared the winner. Chris won thanks, in the main, to his insistence on buying some World Cup Willie memorabilia to celebrate England hosting the 1966 version.

We spent a week in Ireland learning to be Gaelic Football commentators, eventually commentating on the All-Ireland final at Croke Park. It is fair to say he struggled with the pronunciation of legendary GAA commentator Michael O Muircheartaigh. Ok, we both did. He also struggled to make the final. He had to present *Goals on Sunday* before being biked to an airstrip on the outskirts of London, flown by private jet to Dublin and then biked to Croker. We – or should I say I – was already on the air and the game was well underway when he arrived, cool as a cucumber, while I was sweating at the prospects of a solo debut commentary.

The welcome we got in Ireland made me realise how much impact *Soccer Saturday* was having. We were swamped by fans wherever we went, all of them thinking they were the first to shout 'Unbelievable Jeff!' at us. I remember telling him at the time we were like Posh and Becks, though on reflection I was far from posh and Kammy certainly hadn't been anything like Becks in his playing days. He was enjoying the sort of fame he would never have achieved by playing football.

Chris has bottomless energy and would also throw himself into charitable fundraising for the likes of Marie Curie, where he was an ambassador. And he never needed asking twice to support my Prostate Cancer walks.

•

Then, from out of nowhere, it all began to go wrong for Kammy. Sky axed *Goals on Sunday*, though to this day I don't understand why. They certainly had nothing to replace it with. They kept the name alive for a segment shown on *Sky Sports News* but it bears no resemblance to the original. Previously, Kammy would always have been at the biggest in-vision game of the weekend, but now he found himself being sent to Championship or League One fixtures. He covered them with the same enthusiasm as he covered every game.

And there was another thing. His speech was becoming slower, more hesitant, sometimes a little slurred. People were asking hurtfully on social media if he had been drinking.

I knew that would never be the case as Kammy was the ultimate professional and never had a drink on a matchday. But I was aware of the problem and so was everyone else involved with the show. Chris was having to fight to force his words out. It made uncomfortable viewing for everyone who knew him as a man who rattled out his words with machine-gun speed, if not accuracy. The unspoken fear was that this was the onset of dementia caused by heading the football. Former England and West Brom star Jeff Astle was a high profile victim of this and later Gordon McQueen, a former colleague of ours on *Soccer Saturday* suffered the same way. Some of Kammy's ex-team-mates reassured me that Chris never headed the ball when he could avoid it, but despite that I was almost relieved when he revealed he was suffering from apraxia of speech. But if it was perhaps the lesser of two evils, for him it was devastating. After twenty-five years of making people laugh, lighting up rooms with his bonhomie, he had to come to terms with struggling to speak at all. Apraxia basically means that though Kammy knows exactly what he wants to say, it may come out wrongly or not at all. He was told by doctors that there was no cure and no hope of improvement. He was, not unnaturally, in a very bad place.

Kammy was desperate not to ruin his legacy. Though he carried on with some pre-recorded material, the inevitable came early in 2022 when he announced he was leaving *Soccer Saturday*. It must have been heartbreaking for him. It was for me. His final game had been Rotherham against Shrewsbury from League One.

Things got no better despite many attempted treatments. Speaking to him later, he told me that during the worst times he had many dark thoughts. His voice was his life. Without his voice, he was unsure he wanted to carry on. He pulled out of hosting the World's Strongest Man competition and struggled in commentary during *The Games* though when he received the League Managers Association Special Achievement award in front of hundreds at London's Grosvenor House Hotel, the real Kammy shone through as he joked that the £200 Portsmouth had paid to buy him out of the Royal Navy was still the worst money the club had ever spent.

I met him in Central London to talk over his issues for a documentary *Lost For Words* explaining his difficulties and giving exposure to his little known condition. While we were filming, he struggled a little. But if he spoke in a Scottish (or any other) accent the words flowed freely. The same with singing, hence his appearance months later on *The Masked Singer*. It was quite remarkable and reminded me a little of a pupil on the TV series, *Educating Yorkshire*. He had a terrible stutter, but could sing like an angel.

But hand on heart, I felt our days working together were almost certainly over – and he felt exactly the same. How wrong we both were!

Kammy decided to spend a month in Mexico trying out some unlicensed but potentially life-changing treatment. Initially the specialists there were shocked by the extent of his speech loss. But they insisted they could help him. Week after week, my mate reported his improvement. His balance, which had been terribly affected by his illness, was slowly coming back. And best of all his speech was improving to such a degree that on his good days someone who had not known Kammy in the past, would not have thought that he had a real problem.

Such was the improvement that we accepted an offer from UKTV to go on a road trip together. Not just any road trip though. This was an episode of the *World's Most Dangerous Roads*. I suppose after our experience on *Antiques Road Trip*, I might have thought twice. But here was an unexpected chance to team up again with my old mate.

My son Robbie joked the crew could just follow me down the M3. I thought this was a bit harsh, though I admit I can be a sort of hybrid of Lewis Hamilton, Dick Dastardly and a dodgem driver. Rob had been less than impressed when close to home, I (accidentally, honestly) missed the fact that traffic coming in the opposite direction had priority and I had almost forced an oncoming driver into a ditch. The oncoming driver was Robbie.

My record was not unblemished either, with the instructor on my last speed awareness course opening proceedings with 'Nice to see you again Mr Stelling', dripping with sarcasm.

But we would not be terrorising the roads of Hampshire. The plan was to head to Sri Lanka, where we would have to cope with sheer drops, hairpin bends, deep mud, locals with no fear and animals blocking the road. I signed the contract before I watched some of the previous episodes. That was definitely the wrong way round. After seeing Ben Fogle and Hugh Dennis trying to negotiate a mountain road in Peru with the wheels of their 4×4 inches from a terrifying drop, or Stephen Mangan and Lara Ricote careering down a sheer drop in Australia, I was hoping that if Kammy needed to shout for help, he would get the words out bloody quickly! Social media was already awash with rumours that we were getting back together. I had given an interview to the football magazine *FourFourTwo* and was asked which of my ex-Sky colleagues would I like to work with again. 'All of them,' I replied, 'especially Kammy.' This somehow was translated into Jeff Stelling and Chris Kamara are set to work together when the edition appeared.

Our preparation for the trip started with a bang – quite literally. We were sent on a 4×4 training day deep in Hampshire woodland with an ex-army driving instructor. It had been raining for days and the tracks were deep with thick mud, so treacherous that traction was almost impossible to gain. Excuses over! I was first to try and within 30 seconds had lost control. With a sickening thud, my progress was halted by a massive tree. Kammy appeared on the scene immediately, dancing like a whirling dervish and yelping, 'Thanks Jeff, that's taken the pressure off me and the bumper off the car!' I knew then my mate was his old self.

4

DICING WITH DANGER

'Oh my god, it *is* you Kammy!' shrilled an enthusiastic blonde lady as we waited in line to board our flight to Doha en route to Colombo for the *World's Most Dangerous Roads*. 'Pleeease could I have a selfie with you?' Of course Kammy obliged happily. As our selfie-hunter turned away, delighted with herself, she noticed me. 'Oh, you are the other one,' she said with rather less excitement. And so our roles were already defined. I would be Lewis to his Morse, Andrew Ridgeley to his George Michael, Notts County to his Nottingham Forest, Ernie Wise to his Eric Morecambe. I didn't mind. It was just great to be working with my mate again and to witness his improved health.

We met the crew in the Old Fort area of the beautiful city of Galle, right on the southern tip of Sri Lanka. It was 5,500 miles away from Kammy's home in Wakefield but people still recognised him. On the second evening there, the two of us had gone out for dinner. The restaurant manager regaled Kammy with a monologue about how stylish he looked, how cool his sunglasses were and how he walked like a panda! I sat in my polo shirt and shorts, not feeling the same amount of love.

Before we set off to drive one or more of the world's most dangerous roads, we familiarised ourselves with the car and the Sri Lankan Highway Code. This appeared to include: overtaking on both sides is allowed (indeed almost compulsory); stopping at pedestrian crossings is strictly forbidden; use of the horn is required every ten seconds; always maintain a maximum distance of 3 feet from the car in front of you; never use brakes when swerving around another vehicle will do; always try and do your overtaking on a blind bend; always swerve around dogs sleeping in the middle of the road at the last minute (the dogs are fearless, unlike me). Also, never mind the speed limit, always drive as fast as is humanly possible. If Sri Lanka ever has a Formula One team, our local driver Dilshan would make the likes of Max Verstappen seem slow. Astonishingly we didn't see any serious accidents during our stay, and I have seen more dented cars in Paris. But if anyone is planning a holiday on the island they call the Pearl of the Indian Ocean, take my advice – don't even contemplate car hire.

Before our first day of driving, we visited a Hindu temple for a blessing. They believe in re-incarnation. I do not. Kammy stalled the car as we were leaving the temple. After a hair-raising drive through the streets of Galle, we headed into the jungle and some tough off-road sections. It had been raining heavily, making the track even more treacherous than it would have been normally. My job was to navigate. In fairness if I had been navigator, Christopher Columbus would still have been looking for America now. I missed a turning so overgrown and narrow that a mule would have struggled to get down it and instead pointed Kammy straight ahead down a sharp drop, with no clear view of where it ended. My pal's knees were quite literally knocking. Ok, the road was steep and narrow, but just get on with it, I said. He did.

We ended up at the bottom of a severe incline in the front garden of a small dwelling. The track ended there. There was no way forward and no way back and no way of turning round. We were in the cul-de-sac of all cul-de-sacs. The family who lived there came out and gazed in amazement. 'You don't see this every day!' said one of them. We had to call up the rescue squad on the walkie-talkie. The jungle telegraph was working as crowds were now gathering. Eventually, with the help of a tow and a lot of revs, Dilshan managed to reverse it back up the hill. Unfortunately a couple of trees were damaged and so we offered the family some money to compensate. They politely refused, telling us it was the most entertainment they'd had in years. Dilshan drove us to the next hotel, overtaking Lewis Hamilton on the way.

It was 5.30 the next morning when I woke to the sound of Dionne Warwick singing 'That's What Friends Are For' followed by Kammy singing along with it in the room next to mine. It was my turn to drive today. Breakfast was chicken curry, fish curry, dal, fruit and toast. Dinner the night before had been remarkably similar. I was wary of the fruit as much as the curry, having sampled durian at a market. It not only smells like a cross between sweaty gym gear and sewage, and has the texture of toads, but, to me, it tastes like vomit. As you will gather, I was not a fan. I stuck to the toast, wary that the public conveniences during the day's journey might not be five-star and that my tummy deals badly with spicy food. And toads. Our first stop was an elephant sanctuary. Both Kammy and I were looking forward to this as we are animal crazy. He has horses, cats and goodness knows what else. At our peak the Stelling family were responsible for nine cats, three dogs, two guinea pigs, two turtles, a bearded dragon, a rabbit and numerous chickens. We also feed badgers and foxes. My son Matt also once had stick insects, but you could not really tell if they were dead or alive. When we decided they were actually dead, he replaced them with hermit crabs. Again we could not tell whether they were dead or alive. The clue is in the name. We never saw them.

Most of the cats are strays that have turned up over the years including Dave Challinor. We named him after my friend, the ex-Hartlepool and now Stockport County manager. When he turned up on our doorstep, he was a skinny, fluffy, black and white thing. Now he is the shape of a football (the cat, not the manager). A fluffy grey and white feral cat turned up on our doorstep, hissing and spitting. We called it Duchess, due to its posh-cat appearance. My wife Lizzie – who is a cat whisperer – fed it, put bedding out for it and after four or five months gradually coaxed it into the house. Eventually, having had a taste of home comforts, it decided it was on to a good thing and from that moment ruled the roost. It was only later we realised there should have been no 'ess' in the name. We had not dared try and check his undercarriage. Vets' fees are crazily expensive though. When our ginger cat Gilbert was hit by a lorry from the livery yard next door, he was so badly injured that he needed a so-called super-vet to treat him. But it cost £500 just to get a consultation! They rebuilt him, put his head in a brace and kept him in a cage for twelve weeks. It was extremely hard to watch but now you would never guess that anything had happened to him – unless he was to go through an airport scanner.

At the sanctuary, they were trying to nurse some elephant calves back to health. Not all would make it. A lot do though, thanks to the care and attention they are given. More than 160 have been released back into the wild. At feeding time, dozens of animals approach two or three at a time to be fed with milk and greens, the helpers knowing all of them by name. Near the end of our stay a young woman, training to be a vet, approached us. She was so excited. 'I can't believe it!' she said, before voicing a phrase that has never before been used, and probably will never be heard again. 'My three favourite footballers are Ronaldo, Messi and Chris Kamara.' As an afterthought she continued, 'I like you too, Jeff.' I was getting used to this by now.

We successfully drove through a mountain pass on an unmade road. Kammy would frequently jump out to check how much room I had before the Mitsubishi would go tumbling off the edge. I think he felt he was safer out of the car than in it. Our final encounter of the day was with a man called the Snake Guardian. When villagers found a cobra in their home, they could call him in much the same way that in England we call out Dyno-Rod for blocked drains. He would remove the snake and release it safely many miles away. He reckoned he had returned hundreds of snakes to the wilds and had never been bitten. His young son was with him and plans to follow his dad in the family business. It will have to be renamed Snake Guardian & Son! This was a dangerous place. One of our crew was on crutches by now. She had sprained her ankle when she stumbled as she pulled up her pants after having a pee in the jungle. I won't embarrass Sylvia by telling you who it was.

After an exhausting day, we jumped in with Dilshan for the journey to the next hotel, overtaking Sergio Perez on the way.

•

The next day we tackled the Devil's Staircase. This was a series of hairpin bends as we tried to drive up an unmade road, strewn with boulders, with a rock face on one side and a sheer drop on the other. The team had made a recce of the route on a dry, sunny day. Now it was pouring, water was running down the supposed road and the clouds were so low it was like driving in thick fog. Kammy was at the wheel. We negotiated the first few bends slowly but successfully. But conditions were making it impossible. The car would stall and slide backwards towards the cliff edge while Kammy tried to slam on the brakes and pull up the handbrake. Twice we slid to the right, into ditches and needed the rescue crew to help us out. Had we slid to the left, we would now be fertiliser in a Sri Lanka tea plantation. Kammy & Jeff tea! A blend of Yorkshire and PG tips.

Our lives were insured for £10 million each. I kept this quiet from my family in case they decided to spend some of it in advance, but at this stage £10 million didn't seem enough. A Czech hiker was watching all this with fascination. He spoke superb English, one of four languages in which he was fluent. He told us people who speak four languages are called 'Quadlingual'. People who speak one are called English! I was envious of him, not because of his linguistics, but because he was safely on foot. I was not happy and told the TV team that this was no road for a novice in these conditions. I knew they had discussed whether this was an appropriate route in the circumstances the previous evening. For goodness sake, one of the cars had got stuck on the day of the recce – in perfect conditions. A professional driver took over and he too struggled. For once at the end of the day I was happy to get into the car with Dilshan, who overtook Fernando Alonso on his way to the next hotel.

We had been in a couple of hotels that did not serve alcohol and far from the tourist resorts, there were no bars and precious few places to buy drink. Thankfully that night we stayed in Little England, a surreal development, not far from the jungle. This was a cluster of upmarket English-style houses in a gated community that would not have been out of place in Wilmslow. More importantly our hotel, Pedro's, had a bar. After the day we had endured, we needed a drink.

On my final driving day, we headed to see a local football team. It was bedlam. The rain came down in torrents, the pitch was almost underwater. Next to the footballers, a cricket match got underway despite the downpour after an extended version of the national anthem had been boomed out of the PA system. Rain never stops play here it seems. Horses ran wild across both football and cricket pitches. Some of the nation's 1.5 million stray dogs searched for titbits. (My lunch would usually end up in them and I took as much as would fit into a serviette from a breakfast buffet every day.) A band played. A commentator on the public address system got excited as a batsman hit five sixes in one over. We asked the football coach and players about their favourite player. David Beckham was the unanimous choice. His popularity never wanes. Kammy was in his element as he coached the football team. His vulnerability though showed when he went to kick the ball, only to lose his balance and fall. His balance may be better than it was but it is still affected by his illness. He can't, for instance, ride a bike but then again neither can I and I don't have Apraxia.

Leaving the sports ground, we headed for a tea plantation. After all, when I was a boy 'all the tea in Ceylon' was a phrase in everyday use, and yet neither of us had enjoyed a single cuppa while we had been in Sri Lanka (formerly

Ceylon). And we wouldn't at the tea processing plant either. In a room, surrounded by trophies and awards from all over the world, the head tea taster gave his best Jilly Goolden impression, slurping and snorting and finally spitting the tea out. I am not surprised he spat. The tea was cold with no milk or sugar and frankly would not have been served at Mrs Miggins Guest House. Ok, I know I may be a heathen but give me Typhoo any day.

It turned out that it was almost the last drink either of us had. As we left the factory, we took a winding road out of town, following a lead vehicle with one of our Sri Lankan drivers behind the wheel. As usual, he would dive inside and outside vehicles, pull out into oncoming traffic before dipping back inside at seemingly the last moment and accelerate out of trouble if required. I have no idea why vehicles are supplied with brakes as I had never seen them used. My mistake was to try and follow him. As he overtook a single-decker bus on a blind bend, I followed – only to find to my horror a motorcyclist bearing down on me from the opposite direction. I swerved back inside to avoid him, but the bus was already edging out to overtake something on his inside. Once the biker was past, I swerved back to the outside of the road but not before hearing the screeching noise of metal on metal. We had hit the bus – or as I told the producer, the bus had hit us. Bloody Sri Lankan bus drivers! I pulled in to inspect the damage. Incredibly there was not a mark on the car, just a missing wing mirror. As no one in Sri Lanka uses wing mirrors, this was a result. But we were both shaken. I still had to negotiate an off-road drive through floods, tight bends and sheer drops and even though that went well, we both needed a drink – and not cold tea. We jumped in with Dilshan for the three-hour drive to our next hotel. Even though it was dark, he overtook Carlos Sainz on the way and did it in just over two hours.

Our final filming day would end with us climbing Sigiriya Rock, an astonishing 200-metre high column that rises out of the surrounding jungle, with its entrance through a carving of a lion. There are hundreds of steps to the top as tourists and guides alike make their way up to enjoy the wonderful 360-degree views. But getting to the rock rather than up the steps had been our biggest issue. Kammy was at the wheel when we were overtaken and flagged down by a police car. The officer in charge could have a future as a Bond villain. He looked like he was chiselled from the Sigiriya Rock, over 6 feet tall, thickset and with a smooth, totally bald head. He was the first and last Sri Lankan that we had met who hadn't worn a smile on their face. He was seriously interested in the cameras that adorned the car windscreen. He demanded to know what we were up to, what we were filming and if we had permission from the appropriate government department. Finally he was satisfied, though I am sure I heard one of the crew mention another Indiana Jones movie to him (the *Temple of Doom* was filmed there). It was another episode in a week-long shoot that could have made a six-part mini-series, but would be edited down to 47 minutes. The trip was almost over. The final hotel was

25 minutes' drive away. We jumped in with Dilshan, who surprisingly overtook no one.

As we headed for the airport the following day and the long flight home, I asked Kammy where he felt he was at with his recovery on a scale of zero to one hundred. He reckoned seventy-five. On his good days, I think that was about right. The trip was one neither of us will ever forget. But the 12 to 14-hour days were exhausting and took their toll on both of us. On the days when he was desperately tired, I would have thought sixty might have been more accurate as he battled with speech, memory and balance. But the smile never left his face throughout the entire visit – not even when Dilshan offered to be his driver should he and his wife Anne ever return for a holiday. To put things in perspective, a year earlier and he would not have been able to attempt this extraordinary journey, which is a true reflection of how much he has improved. And a 75 per cent Kammy is better than 100 per cent of most of us. Everyone he met, along with the crew he was working with, loved the exuberance and joy he brought to every task.

We arrived back at Heathrow early on a Sunday morning. As we headed through the 'Nothing to Declare' exit at Terminal 4, customs officers nodded and said, 'Morning Kammy, hello Jeff.' Then one of the final pair of officials leant towards her colleague and in earshot asked who we were. 'That's Kammy,' he replied, 'and the other one.'

The Games of My Life

LEEDS UNITED 2 v 1 MIDDLESBROUGH

Elland Road, 5 March 1977

The first 'Game of My Life' featured in this book is the one that shaped my entire future.

But that morning, on a pitch belonging to the local girls' high school in Hartlepool, I was having my own kickabout, my team was leading 7–6 and I had scored a couple – no mean feat as we were shooting into hockey-sized goals. I had clambered over the fence with a bunch of friends that Saturday for our regular play-until-you-drop or until dinner (lunch if you lived south of Yorkshire) was ready. I was twenty-two years old and was reaching the pinnacle of my footballing career in the Hartlepool Sunday League. But playing on successive days wasn't a problem. We would have played every day if we could have, but work, pubs and girls got in the way.

It had been an exciting week for me as I had started a new job. I had left the *Hartlepool Mail* after nearly four years as a journalist to join the news desk at Radio Tees, a few miles away in neighbouring Stockton. A broadcasting revolution was underway with new independent local radio stations popping up like daisies on a lawn and Tees, based in an old water board building in rundown Dovecot Street, was one of them. I had no radio experience and had not expected to get the job when I applied. But not many people did have experience and the white-suited, debonair programme controller Bob Hopton thought I could have what it takes. He was a pretty good judge as later the likes of Mark Mardell, who would go on to be the BBC's North America editor and Helen Boaden, a future director of BBC News, would eventually join me there. But my first five days there had been shadowing other reporters and learning to edit the quarter-inch tape that we recorded on with a razor blade without slicing off a key word or indeed a key finger. I hadn't uttered one single word to the no-doubt waiting public.

We weren't actually allowed to play on the girls' grass and a blue and white police panda van would occasionally stop on the main road that ran alongside the pitch and throw us off. But on this day it wasn't a policeman (there were no policewomen in those days) who interrupted the game. It was my mum. She was at the fence, headscarf tied, floral dress blowing in the wind and waving a piece of sepia coloured paper in her hand. It was a telegram. Telegrams were still being used to deliver urgent messages as quickly as possible. The Stelling family had no telephone at 12 Catcote Road, but the only reasons anyone received a telegram was

usually if there was bad news (I hoped it wasn't) or you
were getting one from the Queen for being a hundred
years old (I knew I wasn't!). I had never been sent
one before and never received another. It read 'Sports
reporter unwell. Go to Elland Road immediately. Cover
Leeds v Boro.'

Both teams were in the top division at the time
and Middlesbrough were the biggest club in the Radio
Tees region. The game would be the centrepiece of
their sports coverage that afternoon and I was being
entrusted with it. There were two immediate problems.
First, I didn't have a car to get to Leeds. My girlfriend
Lynne was the proud owner of an NSU Prinz which
appeared to be powered by a lawnmower engine and
had a top speed of around 50 mph downhill. On our
regular day trips to Durham one incline used to present
a major challenge. Frequently we were seen bumping
up and down in our seats, like a jockey on a reluctant
horse, to try and encourage the car to the top. But I did
not have a telephone to tell her I needed her – or rather
her charming Prinz! It meant a sprint to her home
and the suggestion of a spur-of-the-moment shopping
afternoon in Leeds, which I had painted as a cross
between Rodeo Drive and Fifth Avenue.

We got there an hour before kick-off with crowds
already arriving. With no clue as to how to get in, I
joined the queue for matchday ticket collection only
to be eventually pointed towards the press entrance.

I was greener than a serving of mushy peas. When I did finally gain admittance, I had to work out how I would contact the studio. Mobile phones were still a decade away and even then would be anything but 'smart'. They were the size and shape of a brick with a similar number of functions. But a helpful newspaper reporter, Ray Robertson of the *Northern Echo*, led me to a cupboard where rows of black phones, all with their rotary dial jack plugs dangling, were hanging. Ray showed me to my seat, I plugged the phone in and dialled 100 for the operator. Every report would have to be done via a reverse charge call. Even if a goal had been scored, the same laborious system had to be followed. Dial 100, wait for what seemed an eternity, ask for a reverse charge call, wait frustratedly for the person at the other end to confirm they would pay for it and finally be patched through to the studio to deliver a breathless report.

Not that I needed to be in a rush for a sedate first hour. Even though Leeds boasted the hugely talented Eddie and Frank Gray, Joe Jordan, Paul Madeley, Alan Clarke, Tony Currie and Paul Reaney in their side, they were awful. Boro were managed by big Jack Charlton and were pragmatic in their approach. Their star players David Armstrong and David Mills didn't get a sight of goal. After a couple of leisurely reports lamenting the lack of action, I began to relax. How difficult could this be? Then on the hour Phil Boersma, who had swapped the red of Liverpool for the red of Middlesbrough, crossed and Alf Wood nodded home, just like 50 per cent of all his Boro goals. I jotted down notes as quickly as I could. My fingers rushed for the dial, the numbers 1-0-0 rotating back to their original position agonisingly slowly. The operator could barely hear me as Leeds fans tried to lift their team. Eventually I was through to the studio, where finally the teenager answering the phones for Radio Tees that day bellowed 'Cue!' down the line and I garbled and stumbled my way through my first-ever goal description at warp factor five (some things didn't change throughout my career!)

Six minutes later Leeds were given a penalty. Peter Lorimer, the man with reputedly the hardest shot in football in the 70s, tried to place it but shot over. I was still on the air trying to describe what had happened, when Leeds were given another penalty. Beads of sweat dotted my brow, panicked words flooded out of my mouth in no particular order, as I attempted to describe the foul and the inevitable equaliser as just three minutes after his miss, Lorimer spotted the ball up again. Oh my god, he missed again. Boro still led. With ten minutes left, centre-half Gordon McQueen equalised and I was trying desperately to contact the operator again. I wasn't sure who wanted the full-time whistle most – the beleaguered Middlesbrough defence or the beleaguered cub reporter!

My nerves were shredded. I had been on the air almost continuously in the last half hour. I was as exhausted as the players. The decibel level in one of the loudest stadiums in the country was ear-splittingly high. Then in the 86th minute, McQueen scored again. Above the cacophony, I screamed as loudly as I could to try and get the operator to understand the phrase 'Reverse charge call please!' As I delivered my report, the full-time whistle sounded and the beaten Boro boys slumped to the floor. In the press box, I was doing the same. At 3.00 I had never been on the radio. By 4.45 you couldn't get me off – or so it must have seemed to the people listening. I honestly can't remember anything that happened after the game, but I knew that while the game was top flight, my reporting had been anything but. I would never be a David Coleman or a Peter Jones.

On the Monday, I pushed open the green double doors of the radio station with trepidation. Debbie McCubbin, the receptionist, was wearing her white Tees sweatshirt with a blood red heart printed on the left-hand side. The boss wanted to see me as soon as I arrived, she told me in a soft and sympathetic Scottish tone. I climbed the flight of stairs fearing the worst. I tapped on Bob Hopton's door and went in. I knew it hadn't been great, but whose first time ever was?

'Jeff,' he boomed. 'You are no longer a news reporter. From today, you are a sports reporter.' Neither he nor I knew it, but he had just changed my entire life.

The Games of My Life

The Octopus League was so named because of the
number of teams in it. It must have seemed a great idea
when the league was formed with eight teams. It seemed
less clever as time went on and others joined, to make it
eleven teams. Mind you, BBC Radio News and Sport did
turn up with only eight players from time to time in the
early days which seemed quite apt. I remember more
than once playing centre-half. I suspect the opposition
manager did not need to be Pep Guardiola to realise we
might struggle with high balls into the box.

My senior football career had started out in
Hartlepool as a slinky, will-o'-the-wisp type of attacker.
We called them inside-forwards in those days, playing
off a main striker. I remember scoring on my debut
for St Joseph's Juniors to level the game at one apiece.
The fact that we lost 8–1 only slightly tarnished the
occasion. Soon I would move back to become a box-
to-box midfielder, where my lack of pace would not
be such an issue, and eventually to right-back where

my lack of pace would be even less exposed. Even the fastest winger can't go past you without any legs.

I played in the Hartlepool Sunday League where I earned the nickname 'Chopper', probably due to the manner in which I would compensate for my lack of pace. I remember being sent off once having been involved in a running battle with a winger called Brian Doughty. I had hacked him down relentlessly and he became thoroughly hacked off with me. After one more late challenge, he came at me, arms whirling. I responded in kind. He was a nasty, niggling little bastard and I would rarely if ever bump into him again. Then a couple of years later, he married my cousin! He turned out to be cut from Francis Benali cloth – a nightmare on the football pitch, but charming away from it. At least my team-mates appreciated me. I was named Player of the Year during an end of season tour to Huckelhoven in Germany. We did the journey in style – North Sea ferry crossing followed by a Hartlepool Corporation bus capable of doing about 40 mph down the autobahn. It wasn't quite Wrexham heading for Las Vegas with Ryan Reynolds and Rob McElhenney.

After I moved to London, I learned from my even older, even slower BBC colleague Ron Jones to stay calm. Whenever a ref would lecture him for a late tackle, he would innocently respond in his lovely, lilting Welsh tones, 'Well, I got there as soon as I could, ref.'

We actually became a decent team by Sunday morning standards. Football and boxing commentator Ian Darke, who would later move to Sky and BT, was then at the BBC. He played on the right-hand side in front of me and we developed a sort of telepathic Neville/Beckham type of relationship, though I got forward more than Gary ever did!

On the other side of the defence was Garry Richardson who went on to brilliantly anchor the Sunday morning radio sports show *Sportsweek* for many years. Garry was a decent footballer but developed a habit that he couldn't shake off. Every time the opposition had a throw-in, he would bellow 'foul throw!' at the ref. It got so bad he occasionally shouted it when it was *our* side taking the throw. He could not help himself. This reached its zenith one Sunday morning when Garry took a throw-in. As he launched it, he let out a never to be forgotten cry of 'foul throw!'. It was fully five minutes before either team could compose themselves enough to carry on.

Simon Green, who went on to be head of BT Sport and who was the brains behind *Score*, their version of *Soccer Saturday*, would often play centre-half with Andy Parkinson alongside. Andy is the son of legendary broadcaster Michael Parkinson. While you could never be quite sure what condition some players would turn up in – if they turned up at all – you always knew where you stood with Andy. He was consistently hungover. When we worked together at BSB – the old, ill-fated British Satellite Broadcasting – he was very unwell with booze at one work bash. As caring colleagues we brought him round, gave him copious amounts of water and shovelled him on to his last train home to Windsor. Andy was impressed that so many of his fellow travellers knew him. It wasn't until he got home that his wife pointed out we had helpfully written 'Andy' on his forehead in blue felt tip.

Graeme Reid-Davies played in midfield and was a really good friend. He went on to do really well at the BBC, becoming executive editor of BBC News and Sport until his career suffered a setback. A colleague, Gordon Turnbull, sent him an e-mail telling him that Andy Gray and Jonathan Pearce were being added to their World Cup commentary team. Graeme replied that he thought they were both 'crap'. Unfortunately, the e-mail was sent to several hundred colleagues plus Andy and Jonathan. Graeme had accidentally sent his response to all of them, not just his good friend Gordon.

The rest of the side was made up of reporters, producers and advertising executives while our goalkeeper, Danny, was an actor, which came in especially useful if we were wasting a bit of time near the end of a close match. God, he was good. As an actor! He was a decent keeper too.

We had already won the title by the time we played Civil Service Strollers. In fact we had won all nineteen games. We needed just one more victory to go down in the history books as the Invincibles of the Octopus League. But Strollers were second in the table and no pushovers.

The game was played in monsoon conditions. It was the end of the season, and the pitch by the Thames had long since seen any grass at all. As the rain tumbled, it became a mud bath, unsuited to our pure passing game.

After a goalless first half, the Strollers took the lead. We huffed and puffed but could not score. Our shot at footballing immortality was fast disappearing. Inside the final ten minutes as we attacked down the left, I ventured beyond the halfway line. I was an infrequent goal scorer, but it was a case of needs must. Decent football was impossible now and virtually every other player was condensed in our attacking third. Then like a vision, I knew what would happen. The ball went wide to our winger who found just enough space to centre. I raced in glorious solitude towards the penalty area. The cross came in. It was too far in front of me. As I reached the edge of the box I launched myself full length (ok, stop the giggling) and made the sweetest of contacts. The ball flew past the keeper and into the back of the net, soon to be followed by me. I slid the full 12 yards through the mud like a licorice torpedo. As I untangled myself from the netting and rose exultantly, my team-mates stood bewildered. No one had a clue who it was who had scored. I looked like a swamp monster, covered from head to toe in thick brown mud. Gradually they realised who it was and ran over to congratulate me, though I noted they were not too keen to hug me. It was my best ever goal, though there were not many admittedly, and my best ever personal footballing moment.

Now we were level, there was no stopping us. With moments to go we snatched the winner. We were the Invincibles. And we did what all Invincibles have no doubt done. In true Jack Grealish fashion, we got totally hammered.

5

THE ENTERTAINMENT GAME

'Let's cross live to Fratton Park where there has been a red card, but for who Chris Kamara?

It was 2010 and the start of the most memorable sequence in almost thirty years of *Soccer Saturday* – although no one realised it at the time.

An hour had gone in Portsmouth's home game with Blackburn Rovers when through my earpiece, I was told there had been a sending-off. Thankfully we had a reporter there. And thankfully that reporter was Kammy.

'I don't know Jeff, has there? I must have missed that. A red card?' said Kammy, puzzled.

'Kammy have you not been watching? I haven't. I don't know where this has come from. I have no idea what has happened. What's happened Chris?' I responded and I genuinely didn't have a clue. I had no live feed of the game, just the word of the producer in my ear. But Kammy was there to bring us the definitive news. Or so we thought.

'I don't know Jeff,' said Kammy, now dissolving into nervous laughter. 'I don't know. The rain must have got in my eyes Jeff.'

Soccer Saturday was the icing on the cake.
Quite literally here, baked by family friend Sophie Sanderson.

By now the vidiprinter had confirmed that there had indeed been a red card.

'Chris, Chris,' I said. 'According to our sources, Anthony Vanden Borre has been sent off for a second bookable offence. Get your fingers out and count up the number of Portsmouth players who are on the field.'

Kammy delivered the killer line, 'No, you are right. I saw him go off, but I thought they were bringing a sub on Jeff.' The boys in the studio had tears of laughter running down their faces. Kammy was worried he might be sacked! He need not have worried. None of us realised that this would be one of the defining moments of the *Soccer Saturday* approach to football. It needed to be fun. The clip went viral on social media, Chris was asked to appear on shows in America and Australia. Fourteen years on and more than ten million views on YouTube and yet people still want to hear the story of the day that Kammy missed a red card.

Of course football is a business and a serious one. But it is also a form of entertainment and it has always been my belief that we should treat it that way. Even the most ardent football lover would be hard pressed to sit and watch six hours of po-faced pundits talking earnestly about matches that the viewer could not see. And no one did the fun side of it better than Chris Kamara and Paul Merson.

Kammy could be easily distracted and I took full advantage whenever I could. He was at Upton Park for West Ham against Southampton when I threw to him: 'The second half is underway at Upton Park. Who has started the better, Chris Kamara?' Kammy gazed down at the game, unaware that he was in vision. The producer, Ian Condron, told me there was a technical issue and to move on. But I thought this could be TV gold so I crossed to Kammy again, knowing – or hoping – that he still would not be able to hear. 'The second half is just underway at Upton Park. Who has started the better, Chris Kamara?' Kammy was still blissfully ignorant of what was happening. Again I was told to move on. You must be joking. I went again! 'The second half is well underway (heavy emphasis on the word well). Who has started the better, Chris Kamara?' We got just the response I had hoped for and expected – nothing at all. 'Not a Scooby-Doo, has he?' I smirked.

Kammy was in vision at a Tyne-Wear derby many years ago when a penalty was awarded. When I asked him who he thought would take it, I was surprised at his answer.

'David Santon, I think,' he said.

'Kammy, I can absolutely guarantee you it won't be David Santon,' I replied.

'How can you be so sure?' he asked, looking puzzled.

'Because David Santon plays for Newcastle,' I explained gently, 'and the penalty is to Sunderland!'

Chris provided us with something every week. He coined a new phrase: 'Spurs are fighting like, like . . . beavers'; a new word: 'their energy has dispissipated'; and a new move: 'Speroni is doing turnovers with his feet.'

But I think the best from a collection of thousands of Kammy classics is his goal description – or was it? – from Fulham against Middlesbrough in 2007. We had crossed to him for an update when over his shoulder something happened. To this day, I am not sure what.

'It is Papa Bouba Diop with a header. It is a goal!' he said urgently, looking over his shoulder. 'It's a goal Jeff.' Then the doubts crept in. 'David Healy's running away, the ref Andy D'Urso is playing on. Sorry my monitor is down. I'm looking over my shoulder,' he told us, while looking over his shoulder. 'Don't really know. The assistant hasn't given it,

I don't think Jeff,' he said breathlessly. 'No, the referee hasn't given it either.' By now Kammy's head is on a swivel, from the camera to the game and back to the camera. 'Don't really know what's happening Jeff,' in one of the least required of admissions. Cue nervous laughter. 'Ha-ha-ha. Could be,' he said looking down the lens, then turning his head to the Craven Cottage pitch again before turning back to camera. 'Could be not! Ha-ha-ha.' I still don't know to this day if Papa Bouba Diop scored, but it was unintentional genius yet again from Kammy.

I always thought of Dean Windass as Kammy-Lite. The former Bradford and Hull striker worked on the show for a few seasons. Just as in his playing days, he threw himself heart and soul into everything. His reporting was always excitable. I saw him described once as 'just like a kid who loves his football. He gets incredibly excited when he talks about it.' I think that is a very fair description. Dean was at the Riverside Stadium in Middlesbrough one day when a goal was scored while he was on air. He looked over his shoulder. 'There's been a goal Jeff. Come back to me,' he said urgently. 'Give us a clue, Deano. At least tell us which side has scored,' I pleaded. Dean was never afraid to admit when he didn't know something. Describing a substitution, he helpfully told viewers he couldn't remember who had gone off. He was too honest for his own good.

Like Kammy, Paul Merson often has a vocabulary all of his own. 'They have a dogging midfielder', 'they've shot themselves in the arm', 'that's put the pigeons amongst the cat' and 'if they get a draw out of this, they'll be doing cart-horses' gives you an idea,

One of the low points of my career was when Merse corrected me over a pronunciation. For perspective, he calls Allain St Maximin 'Sam Maximus', Willian 'Will-i-am', Julian Speroni either 'Sebroni' or 'Peroni' or sometimes in desperation 'the goalie' and Michy Batshuayi 'Batswari'. So I was suspicious when he told me I was wrong in pronouncing Huddersfield Town's David Wagner as 'Vagner'. It was pronounced 'Wagner', he told me. Of course he was right. The manager is American/German. I still won't be enrolling in the Merson school of pronunciation any time soon.

Paul is responsible for a story which started on *Soccer Saturday* but where the punchline wasn't delivered until Monday. During the course of the six hours, the *Soccer Saturday* panel consume enough to feed a small African nation. Sandwiches, chips, crisps, chocolate – anything to keep their finely tuned athletes' bodies in shape. Merse had been eating, but was delivering a first-half report when one of his upper middle teeth, weakened by a Sky Sports baguette, flew out. A gap-toothed grin showed the extent of the damage. Our floor manager, Frankie, disappeared but returned during the commercial break with a glass of milk. She told Paul to put his tooth in the milk as it would help preserve the roots until he could get to see a dentist. Daft as it sounds, this is true and not an old wives' tale! The milk keeps the tooth moist and contains proteins that can help. Merse nursed that glass of milk containing the submerged tooth like a baby. He carefully carried it to his car and drove home cautiously with his precious cargo. When he got an emergency appointment at his dentist on Monday morning, he proudly presented the tooth, explaining that he had kept it in milk to preserve the roots all weekend. The dentist fished it out of the milk and looked.

'Mr Merson,' he said. 'This is a false tooth!' Merse had forgotten the original tooth had been knocked out during a match years earlier.

In the early days, much of the fun was down to Rodney Marsh of course. Rodney could be prickly as a porcupine and he invented one-upmanship. If you have been to Tenerife, he has been to Elevenerife. But Rodney made headlines. He was ruthless, cutting and didn't care who he offended. When Bradford City were in the top flight, Rodney said on the show, 'I think Bradford are the worst team ever to play in the Premier League. They are like a cat with a long tail in a room full of rocking chairs. Everywhere they turn, they will get turned over. They have a poor, small stadium. Bradford will get stuffed at some point.'

It was headline news in the local newspaper the *Telegraph & Argus*. In Bradford, he was public enemy No. 1. In fact he was public enemy No. 1 in most places. He had already dubbed Bolton's former Real Madrid star Ivan Campo a pub player. And he had initiated a spat with fellow panellist David Ginola, who he insisted on calling Dave, even when he knew the Frenchman wanted to be called Daveed. But this was the sort of publicity the show needed.

Rodney was so sure in his prediction about Bradford that he agreed to have his head shaved if they stayed up that season. They did just that by beating Liverpool on the final day. Rodney kept his side of the bet and the following season, in front of a capacity crowd, he entered Valley Parade as a blond bombshell and left looking like Telly Savalas. Rod was determined to have the last word though. 'It is like watching a bad American B-movie with someone in the electric chair. Then the gov'nor comes along and gives him a stay of execution. Well, City got their stay of execution last year, but this year they are going down.' Sometimes you could not let him have the last word. Chris Turner, a friend of mine and then Sheffield Wednesday manager, agreed to give us a live interview. At the end of it, Rodney yawned loudly and exclaimed sarcastically 'God, how interesting was he?' 'A lot more interesting than you usually are!' I bit back.

•

I have never worn glasses on TV – I am far too vain. But Charlie Nicholas thinks I should. In 2010, Blackpool missed a glorious chance in the game he was covering against Stoke. Charlie reckoned it would not have counted as the Blackpool player was offside. 'You should have gone to Specsavers, Charlie,' I said. 'He wasn't offside. He was bang onside.' Charlie was riled and buried me with his reply. 'Well, maybe you should go also Jeff, because you couldn't see driving home the other night and you won't wear your glasses on TV in case you get slagged off!' Of course he was dead right.

On another occasion we had a live interview with Sir Alex Ferguson from Old Trafford. The really big-name managers were difficult to get live on the show, but Sir Alex agreed to do it as he was receiving the League Managers Association Manager of the Month award and he is a keen advocate of the LMA. During the course of live interviews, I would generally ask the first two or three questions and the rest of the panel would then weigh in. But Sir Alex can be quite intimidating and only Charlie, who had always got on well with him, had questions to ask. I noticed Phil Thompson sitting on his hands not wanting to get involved in any Liverpool/Manchester United skirmish. It all went well until they started to test the stadium tannoy system. It is often not easy to hear through an ill-fitting earpiece at the best of times, but I could sense Sir Alex was finding this an issue. Then the groundstaff turned on the sprinklers, which were heading perilously close to the great man. By now his mood was changing. I took over again from Charlie and asked one more question. It was a question too far. 'Jeff,' Sir Alex growled. 'You usually ask sensible questions, so why have you asked such a stupid one?' Put firmly in my place on live TV, I responded in the only way I could think of. 'Charlie Nicholas told me to ask it!' I blurted out. I didn't meet Sir Alex often during my years at Sky. But I have to say on the rare occasions our paths crossed, he was always very decent with me. He is also a great raconteur at the dinner table.

Gary Johnson, then Bristol City manager, was always approachable. During a live cross over before a game against

Wolves, he said he would bare his backside in Burton's shop window if one of his players, defender Liam Fontaine, scored a goal. 'Don't worry Jeff,' he said, 'my backside is safe.' Actually it was the good people of Bristol who were not safe. Twenty-seven minutes in, Liam Fontaine put City ahead. 'Time to turn the other cheek, Gary,' I remarked. I am not sure if this contributed in any way to all Burton shops eventually shutting down. The manager – and the people of Bristol – were unlucky. In eight years at the club, the player made 262 appearances and only scored six times!

We crossed live to Adams Park, home of Wycombe Wanderers, where Mark McAdam was speaking to the home manager Gareth Ainsworth. There are three types of managers on matchdays. Tracksuit managers, suited and booted managers and Gareth Ainsworth. Ainsworth was as usual dressed in cowboy style boots, leather jacket and white shirt opened almost to his waist. I didn't know how long I had before the interview would be wound up, but I pulled off my tie, unbuttoned my shirt and pulled it apart. When they handed back to me in the studio I was basically bare-chested à la Ainsworth. 'Gareth,' I said, 'there are only a handful of us who can pull off this look.' I love a bit of mischief on the show and sometimes circumstances presented me with an open goal. As a former Southampton season ticket holder, I didn't enjoy watching Saints lose 9–0 at home to Leicester City in 2019. But I was looking forward to winding up Matt Le Tissier about it during the show. On Twitter, Matt had asked for the day off following the humbling defeat but there was no chance of that. I got stuck into him straightaway, but he deflected my first question. 'Did you see the rugby this morning? We are in a World Cup final and this is all you want to talk about?' England had beaten New Zealand 19–7 that morning in the semi-final. But there was no way I was letting him off the hook. 'The interesting thing Matt is that Leicester scored more than the All Blacks!' Cue hysteria.

Phil Thompson will tell you I can be like a dog with a bone. Daniel Sturridge had dived when playing for Liverpool in a game he was watching. I wanted Thommo to condemn him as a cheat. 'He dived, but he is not a cheat,' Phil insisted. 'Isn't diving cheating then?' I asked. Thommo was defending for his life now, just as he did when he was a player at Anfield. 'When you call someone a cheat, you are talking about people who do it consistently, they are the cheats.' I was having none of it. 'So if someone robs a bank but he only does it once, is he not a bank robber then Thommo?' I asked. The exchange went on and on but there was no way that Phil was ever going to call one of his beloved Reds a cheat. I think it was around that time that we stopped pundits from watching their old clubs, just in case they were a tiny bit biased.

Of course sometimes – lots of times in truth – it was me who looked the idiot. I remember having a go at Lyle Taylor, then with Nottingham Forest, for having his hair dyed a vivid pink. I was mortified when I was told he was doing it to raise awareness of breast cancer as he did every year.

I had met Lyle once at a dinner and thought him a really impressive individual. I had to think of a *Soccer Saturday* way of apologising. So I bought a pink wig and put it on the following weekend. 'Lyle, this is my apology. I look like Boris Johnson gone wrong. So every time you score this month Lyle, this wig goes on!' I honestly can't remember how many goals he scored, but I do know the wig made more than one appearance.

I was in the pink again when Michelle Owen was criticised for her choice of pink trousers when presenting *Monday Night Football*. Michelle is one of my best friends at Sky, so I decided to show solidarity with her by wearing pink trousers on *Soccer Saturday* that weekend. Surprisingly I didn't have any. I was on a trip to Chester with my daughter, Olivia, touring the university. Between us we managed to find a pair of bright pink trousers from Primark. During a commercial break that Saturday, I slipped them on and returned to my desk. Of course our bottom halves are always out of vision, so while it is smart jackets on the top half, most of us usually wear jeans below the waist. Years ago Rodney Marsh would wear shorts, which was ok. Then he would tell us he was going commando, which was not ok! Kris Boyd occasionally wore shorts in recent seasons, but I didn't ask the question! When we got back from the adverts, I told viewers about the unfair comments made about Michelle's trousers and announced I wanted to show solidarity. And I did. But I showed a little more than that.

I hadn't realised how tight the trousers were, and when I stood up there was little left to the imagination. It caused quite a stir on social media. Secretly, I was pretty pleased!

•

With *Soccer Saturday* sometimes the humour had nothing to do with football. I remember the fire alarms at Sky going off half an hour into the show one day. Despite my protestations, we were told in no uncertain terms that we all had to evacuate the building. The next item in the show was an interview with Tony Pulis, who was manager of Stoke City. I linked into the interview and headed for the assembly area. An hour and a half later we were allowed back after the fire brigade had searched the building and decided it was a false alarm. When we got back into the studio, three or four of the firemen asked for photos. Even though I was concerned that the house of some poor soul in nearby Isleworth might be burning to the ground or a cat might need rescuing from a tree in Brentford, I obliged. I even kept them a little longer as I asked to borrow a helmet to wear when we finally came back on the air. I would have made the campest looking fireman in the brigade! My first act was to apologise to viewers. During the 90 minutes that we stood shivering in the assembly area, they had suffered a worse fate. The interview with Tony Pulis had been repeated again . . . and again . . . and again for the full 90 minutes. There's no truth in the rumour that the Americans adopted the method as a new form of torture for those in Guantanamo Bay!

On another occasion my phone rang during the show. The ultimate sin on live TV is of course to have your mobile switched on, so I was being ultra-unprofessional. But, as it was ringing, I decided to answer it. Incredibly the people ringing me live on Sky were Sky. It was the Sky broadband team helpfully asking me if I needed an upgrade. As I ended the call and explained what had happened, I wagged my finger at the camera. 'You need to be more professional,' I said gravely. They really should have rung back and said the same thing to me. I was less than professional too when Bianca Westwood was in danger of being blown away at Dagenham and Redbridge when gale force winds and lashing rain left her clinging to a stanchion just to stay on her feet as he she tried to tell us the referee was taking the players off and abandoning the match. I was only joking when I said she needed to stay where she was as the teams might come back out. When the storm subsided enough for the last few minutes to be played, the referee did indeed bring the teams back out. Bianca was still there, wetter, colder and bedraggled. We were beside ourselves with laughter in our warm and dry studio. I got quite a lot of complaints on social media that day, but Bianca could handle herself. When she was covering a Cambridge United game, I suggested it was the closest she had ever got to university. She actually has two degrees and proceeded to wipe the floor with me – and I deserved it.

Of the current team of pundits, Tim Sherwood has already established himself as a leading member of the foot-in-mouth club. He is one of my favourite pundits, unafraid to say what he thinks, even though what he thinks isn't always right! Tim was watching his old club Spurs try and hold on for a 0–0 against Liverpool at Anfield. When the home side won a corner in the 90th minute, he confidently predicted Tottenham would be able to defend it. 'I am not too worried to be honest. Spurs have been so dominant in the air, I am not sure any Liverpool player can get a head on this (pause) . . . apart from him!' Roberto Firmino had arrived with a towering header. The Liverpool fans erupted into noise, Tim sat very quietly. In the 2022–23 season, he managed to confuse presenter, panel and viewers with his conviction that Preston had a penalty in the first few minutes against QPR. 'It has to be a penalty to Preston,' said Tim. 'A nailed on pen. I can't see the ref so I don't know what has been given but it is a pen.' It needed Clinton Morrison to step in and point out that the Preston player who had been fouled was defending in his own box, not attacking. Tim had forgotten which way Preston were kicking!

Sometimes things that made people at home laugh didn't necessarily make me laugh, usually because it meant Hartlepool conceding in the last minute. During *Soccer Saturday* the idea was always to build to a crescendo of excitement approaching full-time. If a game is close, every fan is desperate for confirmation that their team has hung on or perhaps snatched a late equaliser. In 2015, Hartlepool were bottom of League Two with a handful of games to be played, but under Ronnie Moore were staging what we hoped would be a great escape. Pools were leading Mansfield 1–0. The game had been one of the first to kick off but as the results flooded in there was still no sign of our game ending. It was too much for me. Arms flailing like a policeman trying to control traffic at India's busiest intersection, I pleaded, 'Blow your whistle man in black. It is over. Every other result is in. We were one of the first games to kick off in the second half. It was four o'clock. We have played an hour in the second half. This is crazy. It is dark outside. Blow your whistle man!' I think every football fan can relate to this. Not only did Hartlepool hold on to win, they also avoided relegation. I am still waiting for the club to build a statue of Moore outside Victoria Park.

In the early days of *Soccer Saturday*, I was told a snooty BBC executive dismissed us as 'that comedy show'. We were, I believe, much more than that, but if we made people smile then I am very happy with that.

6

CHANGING TIMES - THE GOOD

When I think back to my dad struggling home from his 6 a.m. to 2 p.m. shift at the local steelworks, pushing his bike, covered from head to foot in grime and dead on his feet, I can't believe how lucky I have been. I have literally lived the dream, reaping the rewards of working on TV but also working on a sport I adore.

I was brought up in a sport-loving family and every minute that I could, I would spend playing or watching.

Our family holidays were spent on day trips with the local bus company to the horse racing at Redcar, Thirsk, Catterick or Ripon. Bets were in pence rather than pounds. I didn't need to look at the racecard. If Geoff Lewis was there, I would always want my money on whatever he was riding. Years later I became the racing reporter on BBC radio, working with the legendary commentator Peter Bromley. Peter was brilliant but a hard taskmaster. Once at York, he barked out a number for me to ring. With Peter you never questioned, you just did it. As the phone was finally answered Peter told me to ask for the clerk of the course,

John Sanderson, one of the most important men in British horse racing. 'When you got him, tell him it's a bloody disgrace. There's no toilet paper in the men's loo and I have had to wipe my arse with the greyhound page of the *Racing Post*.' Right on cue a voice on the other end of the phone said, 'John Sanderson speaking. How can I help?'

Interviewing winning trainers wasn't the easiest either. I remember asking to interview the great Henry Cecil after a big race win along with my colleague from LBC/IRN, Colin Turner. 'Interview each other, why don't you?' came the withering response from Henry. Thankfully in the past couple of decades, attitudes within racing towards the media have changed, thanks in part to the likes of Steve Cauthen, Frankie Dettori, Luca Cumani, the Hannons and many others.

Myself and a friend would play five-day Test matches on the local playing field – just the two of us. When I played for my school I was more Boycott than Stokes. I remember once being dropped from the team after scoring five in nineteen overs. As it was a twenty-overs-a-side game, I had selfishly but unintentionally made sure that most of the other kids didn't get a bat. I wasn't good enough to get into my senior school team until one day, watched by a teacher, I bowled a four-wicket maiden during a house match. He was convinced that I was the next Shane Warne and I was immediately promoted into the first XI. It would be my one and only appearance. As soon as their batsmen had taken a look at me for a couple of balls, they sent my slow, straight, non-spinning deliveries sailing over the boundary time and again.

I enjoyed cricket though and during the summer I would spend afternoons drinking fizzy drinks and filling in my unofficial scoring book at Hartlepool Cricket Club in the North Yorkshire and South Durham League. In those days each club would boast a relatively famous overseas professional. I am sure I saw Lance Gibbs, the West Indian spinner play at Park Drive once.

Aged about thirteen, I wrote to Seaton Carew golf club to ask if someone could nominate and second me as a member. I had played there a couple of times with a friend with my ancient half set of second-hand clubs. But we didn't mix in the sort of circles who played golf so I didn't know anyone who could help me become a member. I was shocked when the club secretary turned up on my doorstep to tell me I had been accepted into their junior ranks. Fifty-five years on, it is safe to say I am no better now than I was then. All the gear, but no idea, I think is the phrase.

My mum and dad used to go to the local working men's club every Monday and Thursday to dance. As well as its social side the club had a thriving boxing section. My dad put my name down to join it. He must have been mistaking me for him. In that very same club he had knocked a man, who had sold me a dodgy car, unconscious with a single punch. And that was on the dance floor, not in the ring. I told him I would rather vote Tory than fight. My father was a staunch Labour supporter so he realised the seriousness of the situation. I might have gone on to be the heavyweight with the shortest reach in boxing.

We went to the local stock car race meetings and watched motorcycle scrambling religiously every Saturday on TV. We would play tennis every evening during the summer months. The only sport I didn't enjoy was rugby union. Aged eleven, I went to Hartlepool Grammar School where they played rugby rather than football. As if that wasn't bad enough as a podgy, overweight kid I was chosen as a prop forward. Years later my son Robbie would show me what I should have done. When he was forced to play, he told them he was a winger. He was so far out of the way, in some games he would not ever touch the ball. But as a prop, you were in the thick of it, getting beaten up or gouged in the heart of the scrum. If you ever did get the ball, you were clobbered by somebody twice your size (not difficult in my case). I hated it. Years later I would join West Hartlepool Rugby Club as a member on the grounds that it had the cheapest beer and attracted the prettiest girls in town. That was great until one Saturday somebody dropped out of the fifth team and I was told I would have to play. I resigned from the club instead.

And of course we played football every minute of the day, after school, at weekends and during school holidays. There were no replica kits in those days so we would turn up in normal button-up shirts or jumpers. Boots came in one colour – black, but most of the time we just wore normal shoes. Trainers were not really a thing until the 70s. The choice of ball was usually between a leather football so heavy that when it got wet it was like kicking a medicine ball and with laces and a valve that could take your eye out, or a Frido, a cheap plastic lightweight ball that Lionel Messi would have had trouble controlling. We loved it regardless but the residents of houses with gardens facing the playing field were not quite as happy as they saw their chrysanthemums trampled as we retrieved misplaced passes (not from me of course) that ended up in their cherished flower beds.

Football has always been my passion. And it is a better game now than when I first fell in love with it. When I first started covering football there were no mobile phones, no internet and Twitter was something the birds did. Apple was a fruit. Electric cars existed but only in Scalextric. The Ford Fiesta was the must-have real car – though you didn't need to wear a seatbelt while driving it and you could fill it up for 8p a litre. A pint of beer would cost you 20p. Music was played at either 33 rpm or 45, streaming was something only associated with a cold. It was a different world so it is no surprise the game has moved on.

For me the single greatest footballing innovation in my time has been the introduction of the play-offs. Before 1987, promotions and relegations could be decided weeks before the end of a season. And even if they weren't, the number of clubs who could potentially go up or down was pretty minimal. For mid-table sides, it was a case of going through the motions in matches that were effectively dead rubbers. Now we often go into the final day of the Championship or Leagues One and Two with six or seven sides still in with a chance of promotion via the play-offs. Of course it is hard to swallow at times. Nottingham Forest for instance failed to go up to the Premier League in 2010 despite finishing three places and nine points ahead of Blackpool, who were eventually promoted. But in 2022 it was Forest's turn to go up by beating Huddersfield – who had finished above them – in the final.

And what games the play-offs have given us. I can still hear Johnny Phillips' brilliant commentary from Vicarage Road as Leicester had the chance from the penalty spot to win a place in the Championship final, only to find themselves beaten within seconds. Watford keeper Manuel Almunia saved Anthony Knockaert's 96th minute spot-kick and follow up, Watford swept down field, Johnny's eyes were popping out of his head as the ball fell for Troy Deeney to smash it home. Cue hysteria. In fact, Johnny had been hysterical for 45 seconds already. It was one of the most memorable moments in play-off history. What is often forgotten is that Watford still didn't reach the Premier League, losing to Crystal Palace in the final.

I hadn't really meant to watch the National League play-off semi-final between Wrexham and Grimsby in 2022. I had just switched on for a few minutes, thinking Wrexham were near certainties to win. It turned out to be one of the greatest games of football I have ever seen, with the underdogs Grimsby, who had twice been behind, winning 5–4 thanks to a goal in 119th minute. It could easily have been 15–14.

My own side Hartlepool were seven minutes away from playing in the Championship when they led Sheffield Wednesday in the 2005 League One final at Cardiff. In desperation Paul Sturrock, the Wednesday manager, was playing a system that looked like 2–2–6 to try and get an equaliser. They did, as our centre-half Chris Westwood conceded a penalty and was sent off (it was a ridiculous decision, but I am almost over it now). Our ten men hung on gallantly to take the game to extra-time but Wednesday's numerical advantage saw them through.

Gillingham were 2–0 up against Manchester City in the 1999 third-tier final with a minute to play, only for Horlock and Dickov to score last gasp goals to take the game to extra-time and a shootout that City would win. Without their astonishing great escape, City's history might have looked very different, who knows? And Sunderland's Micky Gray will not want reminding how missing the fourteenth penalty of a shootout allowed Charlton to win the Championship final of 1998. That miss has become more talked-about than Clive Mendonca's hat-trick in the same game.

Micky may not agree but penalty shootouts are another of the great footballing innovations of my life. People call them a lottery, but at least there it is a test of skill and nerve. I am old enough to remember when games were decided by the ultimate lottery, the toss of a coin. Liverpool reached the semi-finals of the European Cup in 1965 thanks to Ron Yeats calling heads against Cologne (It may not have been heads. To be honest I am guessing but I have a 50/50 chance.) Domestically, FA Cup ties were played to a finish even if it took eleven hours and six replays, as was the case when Alvechurch played Oxford in 1971. It didn't just affect the minnows either. Arsenal and Liverpool played four times in the 1980 semi-final before Brian Talbot finally edged the Gunners home.

I have never understood why some people want to replace the penalty shootout. I know it ends in heartbreak for one side – usually England. But for drama there is nothing quite like it. Gareth Southgate, Chris Waddle and Stuart Pearce might not agree – but I think they would. The only downside for me is that many teams play for penalties rather than trying to score outright winners, especially during the second period of extra-time. But the alternatives like a 'Golden Goal' turned out to be dull and anti-climactic. A word of warning though. You can have too much of a good thing. Last year Manchester United beat Arsenal 2–0 in a pre-season friendly in the USA. Yet there was still a penalty shootout at the end. This is the daftest idea yet from the country that gave us a World Series in which only North American teams take part and a football league without promotion or relegation.

Given a chance the Americans would probably scrap the offside laws completely in the hope of encouraging more goals to be scored. In fairness the changes to offside over the decades have benefited the game too. No one would want to see a return to the days when a centre-forward's 30-yard volley that dips just under the crossbar could be ruled out because a winger standing 25 yards away and almost in the crowd was in an offside position. But I do think something has to happen about officials getting out their set squares and protractors to chalk off a goal because the attacker has a bigger boot size than the defender.

Just as winklepickers, kipper ties and clover leaf lapels have gone out of fashion (ask your dads), so has the up-and-at-'em style of football. Do I want to see Manchester City build from the back starting with a Cruyff turn from Ederson? Yes I do. Do I want to see every team try and do it, even when their players are less capable? Well, probably yes again as it results in so many almighty cock-ups, but I wouldn't if I was a fan of the team. By the way, goalkeepers have changed too. In the 70s Les Green at Derby and Lawrie Sivell at Ipswich were both 5 feet 8 inches tall – above average height for a man. They played well over 200 games between them. Now if you are under 6 feet tall you are thought of as being too short to be a keeper.

The game is much less physical these days, possibly too much. I don't want it to become a non-contact sport, but I also don't want a return to the Chelsea v Leeds United FA Cup final of 1970 where it was almost a case of last man standing collects the trophy.

The increase in the number of sides who can go up or down in the English leagues has in fact been another positive step. In my boyhood, two-up and two-down was the norm and if you finished in the bottom four of the Football League, you had to apply for re-election rather than being automatically relegated. This is one area where my team are record holders (in all honesty the *only* area in which they are record holders). They were re-elected successfully fourteen times – more than any other club. It was the ultimate old pals' act. A dozen games from the end of one season we appointed a new manager – not for what he knew, but for who he knew. Sure enough we finished in the bottom four but he was able to lobby his contacts to ensure we stayed in the League. Thank goodness that there is now automatic promotion and relegation between League Two and the National League. It does not go far enough though. The fifth division in English football is now predominantly full-time and sides that are promoted usually more than hold their own. In my opinion, a third promotion place to the EFL from the National League is long overdue.

There are so many other areas where strides have been made. Before 1965 there were no substitutes in English football, now there's a small private army of them on the bench every game. It is frustrating when they are used tactically of course to run down the clock, but it is far better than the days when teams would finish with eight, nine or ten men due to injuries. The alternative would be to tell your centre-half with a broken arm to go and play on the wing. Trust me, it happened.

One of the biggest changes is ongoing. When I go on holiday to Portugal these days, the wonderful wide sandy beaches are awash as always with youngsters practising their ball skills. The difference is that now half of them are girls! I remember a decade ago seeing an eleven-year-old girl rinse the defenders during one of my sons' Sunday morning games. In those days seeing a girl play was about as common as a solar eclipse. Now at grassroots level that is changing and, as the years go by, the standard of women's football will, in my opinion, sky-rocket. We keep hearing stories of top women's sides being heavily beaten by male under-15 teams and suchlike. But the female game is a different game – and none the worse for that. It is competitive, feisty but obviously less physical, though I have seen a punch or two thrown. The women are also catching up with some of the more unsavoury aspects of the male game – Lauren James' stamp on the back of her Nigerian opponent in the last World Cup is evidence of that. But of course, they are not going to be able to compete against male teams.

In tennis Serena Williams would never have been able to beat a decent male player. But we still appreciate her skills in the women's game. In golf, Annika Sorenstam would never win a major against men, but that doesn't make me less likely to watch the Solheim Cup. Florence Griffith Joyner would not have qualified from the heats in the 1988 Olympic 100 metres if she had been running against men. But it doesn't devalue her gold medal in the women's event.

I still know men who say they wouldn't cross the road to watch a women's football match. It is probably just as well as they would risk being hit by a car. They are so blind.

7

AND THE NOT SO GOOD . . .

Most people will tell you that I like a moan. I moan about the Government. I moan about the Opposition. I moan about the disgraceful profiteering of energy and fuel companies. I moan about rail prices and flight delays. I moan about slow internet. I moan about bad drivers (which is rich coming from me). I moan about scaremongering newspapers ('We are all going to drown as sea levels rise' – that's if a meteorite heading on a collision course with earth or a new scary strain of Covid doesn't wipe us all out first). I moan about hopeless boxing judges. And who in this country doesn't moan about the weather – it is too hot/cold/there's a drought/there are floods. I moan about people who pronounce their 'th's' as 'f's'. A trivial fing, but irritating nevertheless.

Football has brought me so much joy throughout my life – probably the first time you have ever heard those words from a Hartlepool fan. But for all the good changes that have happened to the game during my lifetime, there have also been some less welcome developments. For me the resurgence of tribalism in football has been one of the worst.

When I was a teenager I would go to a game at the Victoria Park, Hartlepool and watch the first half from the Rink End, named after the long demolished Queen's Rink ballroom where co-incidentally my mum and dad first met. Then at half-time I and all the other Poolies would make our way to the other side of the ground, the Town End. We would pass the opposition fans making the journey in reverse on a narrow walkway. There might be some lively banter but nothing more. From time to time, we would stay at the Rink End just to pass the time of day with fans from exotic places like Barrow, Halifax or Walsall, something that would almost certainly never happen these days.

I am not seeing all this through rose-coloured spectacles. Going to football in the 70s and 80s was often an unpleasant experience. When I first went to work in London as a radio reporter, I dreaded being sent to West Ham, where the National Front would be touting their poisonous views along the route to Upton Park from the nearest underground station. I was sent to Stamford Bridge to report on Chelsea against Sunderland one evening. Chelsea was swish even then, but their supporters had a reputation for violence. Rumour was rife about where Chelsea thugs planned to lay in wait to ambush the North East fans after the match. Worryingly for me, it was right on my route home and only a heavy mounted police presence helped prevent anything major. And covering Millwall against West Ham was like working in a no-go area. I groaned when I saw that I was being sent to South East London for this one. Forget the threatening atmosphere of La Bombonera and Boca Juniors, this was far more intimidating. It was a night game under the lights. I don't think I had ever seen more policemen or police horses. Overhead helicopters circled, as their search-lights tried to pick out trouble spots. Inside the ground even the media weren't safe as objects whistled down on to our heads from behind. Worryingly it was the directors' box that was directly behind us. I would like to think nothing was thrown from there, but I have my doubts. No wonder women and families were rarely seen at football.

These days there are plenty of women and families at games. But I do fear that the game remains too tribal. My family had three season tickets at Southampton until recently. We were surrounded by lovely people at St Mary's, mainly regulars, with whom we would chat before the game and at half-time. I remember though, that during a home game against Arsenal, a young eighteen or nineteen-year-old fan removed his jacket to reveal his Gunners shirt. The Saints fans turned to seething sinners and abused him appallingly. He was removed for his own safety. But the worst thing was that none of the usually level-headed, good-natured Southampton fans thought they had done anything wrong. In their eyes, the Arsenal fan was the guilty party. And so we have segregation at grounds and at pubs, even occasionally at service stations. And we accept it!

Gone too are the days when most fans watched football with a sense of perspective or fairness. Now if a call goes against their team many fans still claim it is obviously a wrong decision no matter how blindingly obviously correct it was. During the 2023 League One play-off final against Sheffield Wednesday, Barnsley had a 100 per cent penalty turned down. You did not need to have been to Specsavers to see it, yet VAR did not intervene. Two minutes later VAR did intervene to send off Barnsley's Adam Phillips. I was watching as a total neutral and tweeted that the officials had got the decisions horribly wrong in my opinion. Every Sheffield Wednesday fan accused me of still being bitter about Hartlepool's defeat by them in the 2005 League One play-off final! By the way, if I was bitter about sides that had beaten Pools, I would harbour grudges against pretty much everyone.

In 2023 when QPR manager Gareth Ainsworth was suffering personal abuse after his side lost their opening game of the new campaign 4–0 at Watford, I tried to defend him on social media. After all, he had done excellently in charge at Wycombe Wanderers and had been an ex-player and twice caretaker manager at Loftus Road. Perhaps fans should show him some loyalty, I suggested. The response was furious. 'He only gets called a c*** – it's not abuse,' said one. 'He is a tosser,' said the next. Sheffield United fans weighed in condemning Ainsworth for a tackle that ended the career of Dane Whitehouse in 1997, twenty-six years earlier. Many of those criticising were either not alive or not old enough to have been at the game, but their tweets were full of vitriol. Whitehouse said he had never received an apology,

Ainsworth claims he wrote a letter. I don't know the truth but I do know that football should be a game we can savour together, a common passion, not something that fuels hatred.

Usually the one-eyedness of fans doesn't result in anyone getting hurt. That might not have been the case when Roma fans threw chairs at ref Anthony Taylor and his family at Budapest Airport after their Europa League final defeat by Seville. The game had been littered with thirteen yellow cards and almost as many incidents involving Jose Mourinho and his backroom team in the technical area. Later the Roma manager claimed Taylor 'seemed Spanish'.

Afterwards though Mourinho overstepped the mark of what is acceptable when he approached Taylor in the car park as the referee prepared to return to his hotel and called him 'a fucking disgrace'. This was caught on video and soon appeared on social media.

To borrow the slogan of the credit card company that he promotes, that will not do nicely, Jose. His comments inflamed the situation and incited fans already harbouring a misguided sense of injustice. Taylor was lucky not to be hurt. Mourinho was lucky not to be banned for a year. Personally I think managers should not be permitted to comment about a referee's performance at all. Leave that to the TV pundits. Some managers, rather like some fans, are incapable of giving an unbiased view.

Tribalism is one reason why I am one of the few people in football who likes half-and-half scarves. Anything that shows football is only a game, a shared passion that should kindle rivalry but not enmity, has to be a good thing.

•

I don't like the drift of players to Saudi Arabia, where the human rights record is so bad. Of course the money is immense, but most of those who have gone were already earning huge amounts compared to a normal working person. They were not struggling to put food on the table or pay the rent. They are not guaranteeing their family's future. They already had privileged lives. How badly would a nation have to behave for people to make a moral stand? Clearly, politically motivated killings, mass executions, amputations for robbers, lashes for other offenders, no freedom of speech and no recognition of LGBTQ+ rights isn't enough in many people's eyes. The Saudis will have to do something really bad to make some turn down the millions on offer. Thank goodness for the likes of Andy Murray, who rejected a seven-figure offer in 2022, to go and play tennis there. The number of clubs in the Premier League under American ownership is also concerning. Obviously the promotion and relegation system which makes our pyramid so wonderful, is an anathema to some of them who are looking to protect their assets. But the day we scrap them is the day I will turn to *Love Island* or *Married At First Sight* for my entertainment instead.

I certainly don't think VAR has added to the entertainment value of football. In the Premier League every player and fan has to wait before they can truly celebrate. I am not totally against the use of it, but the PGMOL really got it terribly wrong in the first couple of years of its implementation. Talk of 'high bars' is simply an excuse when they get it wrong. A foul is a foul. And their insistence that they stick with the on-field referee's decision wherever possible is simply nonsensical. All they should be concerned about is coming to the correct decision, not protecting the man in black. It is a tough job, performed in a harsh spotlight. Sticking with an obviously wrong decision actually undermines not just the referee, but the whole system. Worse still, we get the situation where the VAR is intentionally protecting his mate in the middle as Mike Dean admitted after he had resigned as an official. He claimed he had not sent Anthony Taylor to the screen at Stamford Bridge when Tottenham's car crash centre-half Christian Romero pulled the hair of Marc Cucurella inside the box, because his pal had suffered a difficult day and he didn't want to add to his grief. I had to read this twice. What a shameful admission from someone who had been one of England's top officials. Remarkably, Mike gives his views on refereeing decisions now on *Soccer Saturday*. After that, how many fans could trust his opinion, do you think?

Even with the much respected Howard Webb in charge, things continue to be as bad as ever, illustrated by the VAR Darren England and his sidekick Dan Cook failing to correct referee Simon Hooper after he erroneously ruled out Luis Diaz's goal for Liverpool against Spurs. Diaz was clearly onside so the decision should have been overturned and the goal should have stood. But for some inexplicable reason, England thought that the referee had awarded the goal and simply confirmed that the check was complete. Hooper, thinking his decision was correct, allowed play to go on. Even when the VAR realised his mistake, like a rabbit in the headlights, all he could say was play has restarted. When the audio of what was going on in the VAR hub was released, it honestly sounded like a booze-up in a bar with people shouting their views but with no semblance of there being a process. VAR was introduced to cut out human error. If ever there was an example of how badly it has failed, that was it.

I don't know how to put it right, but I do know that there should never be a junior official at VAR headquarters in Stockley Park being asked to pass judgement on someone more senior who is refereeing the game. They are never going to overrule. Nor do I believe having ex-players involved will necessarily help. Just look at how often the *Soccer Saturday* panel disagree over a VAR ruling. It takes long enough to reach a conclusion as it is without having an extra voice giving an opinion. I don't want referees to have to explain their decisions after a game to the media either. No one is going to want to hear from them when they have had a good game, but they would face the Spanish Inquisition if they have blundered. I don't see how that improves the game one jot. When I met England World Cup winner Sir Geoff Hurst, his view on VAR could not have been more clear. 'It is crap,' he told me. Perhaps surprisingly though, bearing in mind his third goal against West Germany in the 1966 final, he was very much in favour of goal-line technology. Had it been in use then, he believes it would have proved his second goal – England's third – was inches over the line!

The only thing I have ever liked about the transfer window is Jim White's yellow tie. Actually, to be honest, I don't like that either! The window has been with us for more than twenty years and was initially introduced to stop players, like other workers, being able to give a club three months' notice and then walk away for nothing. Frankly, I would not like my employer dictating when I could or could not leave! The window would also, in theory, mean managers could spend their time coaching – or golfing if they preferred – rather than having to deal with unsettled players, fend off agents or look for new signings themselves for the bulk of the season. It also meant in theory that if a club suffered injuries, the inability to immediately buy a replacement would see younger players more likely to get a first-team opportunity. Previously a club could buy or sell at any time of the season until 31 March.

There are so many things wrong with the current system. If there is going to be a window, surely it has to close before a ball is kicked in a new season, otherwise managers are still left dealing with unsettled players, fending off agents and looking for new signings themselves. A last-minute transfer can leave clubs suddenly short in a key area and unable to replace a player for months. A last-minute deal collapsing can leave players marooned and frozen out, as happened to Hakim Ziyech at Chelsea. It also means smaller, cash-strapped clubs cannot cash-in on an asset outside the windows no matter how desperate their financial plight might be. By the time the next window comes round, that player may have been injured, lost his form or been banned for gambling offences!

On deadline day itself, logic often goes out of the window to be replaced by desperation as the clock ticks round. Prices become wildly inflated and clubs are often left with an overpriced, overpaid dud on their hands. How else could you explain Chelsea paying £51 million to Liverpool for Fernando Torres? Or Stoke coughing up £18 million for Giannelli Imbula? What about Fulham paying £11 million for the Greek, Konstantinos Mitroglu? Mido went to West Ham on deadline day, Alfonso Alves to Middlesbrough, Benjani to Manchester City, Juan Cuadrado to Chelsea, Eric Djemba-Djemba to Aston Villa. The list is endless. The only parties to benefit from those deals were the selling clubs and the agents. I reckon it is time for Jim White to give his yellow tie to a charity shop, send back his mobile phone and for us to return to year-round free movement of players.

•

I know football is entertainment, but whoever thought it was a good idea to have some wobble-voiced warbler singing the national anthem before cup finals?

And please, please, please can we stop blasting out bloody 'Sweet Caroline' at every opportunity at matches.

At the National League final against Hartlepool at Ashton Gate, some finger-happy person decided to play it when Torquay thought they had scored early on, only for the goal to be disallowed. Neil Diamond was cut off mid-chorus, poor Torquay fans were left choking back their words and the DJ (are they still called that?) was presumably suitably embarrassed. 'Sweet Caroline' is an American song written by an American singer-songwriter so I am not sure how it has become an unofficial anthem of our national game. It drives me mad. It is not even his best song. Now if it were 'Love on the Rocks', 'Hello Again' or 'I Am, I Said' . . .

The Games of My Life

BLACKBURN ROVERS 0 v 0 COVENTRY CITY

Ewood Park, 28 September 1997

'You are fucking lucky you haven't been sacked on the spot!' spat the fierce Scottish voice down my earpiece. Thankfully it wasn't directed at me, but at one of the young assistant producers who was working on that day's *Super Sunday*. His sin was to edit a bumper – the piece you often see leading into or coming out of a commercial break – in which you could clearly see one of the players silently mouthing the word 'Fuck'. This was a cardinal sin. Andy Melvin, the producer, was incandescent with rage.

In fairness, Andy was often incandescent with rage. He was an outstanding producer, demanded the best possible product and was determined that there would be no cock-ups on his watch. But in achieving this he scared the pants off a lot of the people he worked with – me included. In fact I am still a bit afraid writing this! He was old school and none the worse for it. I am sure coming through the ranks in Scotland, HR were just two letters of the alphabet. Of course it would be impossible to behave in that manner in this day and age.

Years later, I attended a dinner and discovered I was sitting next to him. I swapped over his place name with another, congratulating myself on my quick thinking. I didn't realise Andy had already been to the table and knew exactly where he was supposed to sit. 'Who's moved these fucking places around?' he demanded. It didn't take much working out. It wasn't until years later that I realised how important he was to the company – he eventually became No. 2 at Sky Sports – and how many careers he had helped with his no-nonsense attitude, mine included.

This was my first *Super Sunday*. Richard Keys had hosted the show since its inception and had never missed one. I don't recall the reason for his absence, but earlier in the week Vic Wakeling had told me I would be presenting that day. It wasn't a big game by Premier League standards but it was a big thing for me to be only the second person to front the programme. And make no mistake, Keys was a hard act to follow. In my view he was an outstanding presenter and his partnership with Andy Gray had been invaluable to Sky in the years after the company had won the Premier League TV rights.

People often ask me what Richard is like. To be honest, I don't really know. Our paths rarely crossed.

He had been a presenter at TV-am when I joined as a reporter, and of course was well established at Sky long before I arrived. He had always been at least one rung above me in career terms.

I got the impression though that he may not have been the easiest to work with when the floor manager asked me which brand of mineral water I wanted in the studio and did I need my shoes cleaned before we went on air that afternoon!

I had arrived in Blackburn shortly before 11 the previous night, driving up the M1 and M6 after that day's *Soccer Saturday*. I was knackered after six hours on the air and the last thing I needed was a four-hour plus drive, but I consoled myself with the thought of a pint or two when I got there. After I checked in, I headed straight for the bar for a beer and some football talk with the team. As I was walking in, they were all walking out. Andy apparently had an 11 p.m. curfew on drinking the night before a programme. And I was told I needed to be onsite at Ewood Park the next morning at 8 to run through the show! On *Soccer Saturday* as long as I was on set 15 minutes before we went on air I was ok. Here I was required eight hours before we went on air. When I rolled up for my big day at around 8.30 a.m., I was greeted with 'Yer Late!'

The rest of the day dragged to be honest. There was a short build-up that didn't take too much planning from my point of view. But there were VTs to be viewed, graphics to be checked, camera shots to be examined, pre match interviews to be recorded and so on. Andy was a perfectionist. Nothing would go to air that wasn't correct. I would be lying if I said my pulse wasn't racing a little faster as we went on the air. Mind you, mine was probably the only pulse in the nation that was beating faster. There had never been a goalless draw between the two sides – until this one. It was a dreary game, enlivened only by red cards for Blackburn's Jason Wilcox and, of all people, Dion Dublin of Coventry. God knows what pundits like Tim Sherwood or Chris Sutton would have said if they'd had to sit through it. They didn't – because they were both playing in it.

I am sure no one who was there or watched it on TV, remembers it at all. But for me it was a landmark day. I don't remember ever replacing Richard again on *Super Sunday*, but years later I would take over Sky's Champions League coverage from him and that often meant being at Barcelona or Bayern Munich. But Blackburn was a significant step along the way for me.

The Games of My Life

ARGENTINA 0 v 1 ENGLAND

World Cup Group F match, Sapporo, Japan, 7 June 2002

Chris Kamara, *Soccer Saturday* producer Ian Condron and I were turning Japanese.

We had learned to queue in an orderly fashion for the bullet train, realised that Love Hotels were nothing to do with a room-booking site and discovered that gentlemen's clubs were just that – a club with no women allowed in.

I had always wanted to go to a World Cup and always wanted to visit Japan. I had been to Thailand and Korea and had loved both. I knew from being at Olympic Games, Commonwealth Games and World and European Athletics championships that places were magical at times of big sporting events. I didn't really fancy a solo trip so asked my friends if they wanted to join me. Two did – a high percentage in truth of my total tally of mates!

I had done a lot of the booking of hotels and flights for our three-man trip, but we had left Kammy to arrange our Tokyo hotel. With prices sky-high and being cost-conscious, he booked a triple-bed room for the six nights we were staying in the Japanese capital. As an ex-professional player, Kammy was used to sharing a room but for me this was a step too far. As I lay in the bath one morning, Chris came into the bathroom for a shave. He was stark bollock naked. My face was inches from his hairy backside and other even less attractive parts of his anatomy. I knew I needed to get out – not just of the bath but the hotel room! From then on I was happy to pay the single supplement.

The Argentina game was the third game of our trip to the 2002 World Cup. We had already seen England's uninspiring 1–1 draw in the opening game with Sweden in Saitama. With many bars and restaurants closed due to the fear of football hooligans, it hadn't been the greatest start to our self-funded adventure to the Orient.

But that changed with the second game. If Japan was ready for football hooliganism, it wasn't ready for the Republic of Ireland's green army, as we found out as we travelled to Niigata for their opener against Cameroon. Japanese society was so orderly that when the home nation won for the first time in the World Cup, thousands of fans ran through the streets, waving their national flag in celebration. But from our perch on the balcony of an eight-storey bar, we saw them, to a man, stop in their tracks. As they raced towards a pedestrian crossing, the green man turned red. Not one person stepped out even though the road was deserted.

Not that the Irish fans were disorderly, but nothing
– certainly not a red man at a pedestrian crossing – was
going to stop them having the time of their lives. The
train for Niigata left Tokyo at around ten in the morning
for the four-hour trip. By eleven, the Irish fans had
drunk it dry – beer, spirits, wine, sake, the lot.

We stood behind the goal with thousands of Irish
supporters and when Matt Holland equalised in the
second half the cacophony was deafening. One of
the green army flung himself from the crowd above,
confident that his fellow fans would catch him when
his short, wingless flight ended. His faith was justified.
Later, we celebrated the 1–1 draw at Church with ref
Dermot Gallagher. Like us, Dermot had paid his own
way, partly to study refereeing performances in the
hope of improving his own, but also to have a good
time. We did that at Church, the all-night bar/club
in Niigata where every football fan gathered. Even
Kammy's karaoke version of 'Brown Eyed Girl' or my
rendition of 'Boys in Green' failed to dampen the mood.

We hadn't been sure we would be able to get a ticket
for the must-see game against arch-rivals Argentina,
but Kammy made some calls and managed to get three,
though he wasn't sure what part of the ground they
would be in.

So the day before the match, we flew to Sapporo on
All Nippon Airways, only slightly perturbed by the fact
that the screen at the front of the aircraft showed no

movies, just the entire flight from take-off to landing. It was like being in the pilot's seat, worryingly with co-pilot Kamara alongside me.

We were looking forward to a night on the town – after all this was Sapporo, home of one of the best beers in the world. But the city was quiet. News that the arriving hordes of football fans came in peace had not reached this northern outpost on the island of Hokkaido, or so it seemed. In the end, we settled on a near-empty first floor bar with a balcony overlooking the main street. We drank and listened to the owner/barman's musical choice. 'Return to Sender', 'Wooden Heart', 'Jailhouse Rock', 'Blue Suede Shoes' – it was Elvis followed by Elvis followed by more Elvis. The owner had the largest collection of Elvis records in Sapporo, probably Hokkaido and possibly even Japan.

Being Japan of course, there was a karaoke mic as well. You had to be there to truly appreciate our new friend's rendition of 'Are You Lonesome Tonight'. Amazingly, he had once landed a recording deal himself, though I imagine he would have found the American and UK markets tough to break. It turned into quite a night and we promised we would return the following evening after the game, only to be told he wouldn't be opening the bar as he was afraid of any after-match violence. The solution was simple. We were giants in Japanese terms – yes, even me – so we would be his bouncers. We would choose who could come in and who couldn't! Suitably reassured, another Sapporo singalong was guaranteed the following night.

The match was at the space-age, spectacular Sapporo Dome, built specially to host the World Cup. We found our seats in one corner of the ground. It had a very American feel to it with vendors everywhere selling snacks and drinks. You could have been at a baseball match and in fact the stadium went on to be used as the home venue for a local baseball team. In front of us was Susan Davies, wife of FA high-flyer David Davies and alongside her was Nancy Dell'Olio, then girlfriend of the team manager Sven-Goran Eriksson. Kammy had gone right to the top for tickets and we were in the VIP zone.

The iconic moment of the game and the tournament from an England point of view was at the far end from us and I honestly had no idea whether Michael Owen had gone down easily under the challenge from an Argentinian I knew nothing about, Mauricio Pochettino. It didn't matter. David Beckham scored and we celebrated like we had won the World Cup. I remember joyfully kissing Nancy and being thankful Sven was busy with the match! The second half was one of the longest I have known. I spent as much time with my eyes on the stadium clock as I did the game as England repelled wave after wave of Argentina attacks with David Seaman outstanding. But we did it. We had beaten Argentina, taken revenge for the Hand of God and surely would now inevitably go on to lift the World Cup.

But the night was young. As we arrived back into the centre of Sapporo, Elvis was opening his bar. As 'Suspicious Minds' blasted out in the background, we stood on the balcony, beckoned some people inside and told others not to bother. Within half an hour, the place was full: Elvis, as we called him now to his delight, me, Kammy, Condo and around forty women! There wasn't even a hint of trouble.

8

YOU BET

'I am so glad to have finally put pen to paper to you, Jeff. I've got to tell you, because you obviously don't realise it, but you are a disgrace!!! How can you sit in your studio on a Saturday afternoon, grinning from ear to ear and making jokey, blokey fun with your mates as the goals go in? Isn't Paul Mercer (sic) one of those mates often? You know what I am talking about – yes, your betting adverts on TV. You are a total disgrace to yourself, your colleagues (you know better than them), to the world of football and beyond. Are you an idiot? Or just a person with no morals or ethics, who makes money out of people's misery? One person dies every day of suicide caused by gambling in the UK. I knew one. How do you sleep at night, Jeff? Sorry if you thought this was a thank you card or early Christmas wishes!'

The card containing this message arrived along with a lot of 'Good Luck' and 'Thank You' cards shortly before I left Sky. I could not help but wonder if he had said the same thing to Roy Keane for his role in recent Sky Bet adverts or

Ray Winstone who promotes Bet365? But in fairness to the writer, he had included his name and address.

I am fortunate that I get very little criticism compared to many on TV. But most of what I do get is in relation to my work for Sky Bet. Another critic – anonymous this time – called me a loathsome individual, greedy, self-centred, and accused me of assuaging my conscience by appealing for donations in support of prostate cancer. I know that in some people's eyes, it may seem incongruous that while I try to publicise good causes, I promote Sky Bet. And I understand that viewpoint, though not so much those who write or post on social media anonymously. I am not too sure though why they can't make the point without using words like c*** or w*****.

I have been betting ever since I was old enough to do so, but always with £5 or £10 stakes at the most. I have never had a bet of more than £100 in my life. It's thrilling when your bet comes up. I remember a horse I had a share in, Beautiful People, winning at 8/1 at Fontwell Park. I remember having £10 on a 33/1 Cheltenham winner. I recall backing six horses in the Triumph Hurdle one year when you were paid out for a place in the first six – not one of mine made that first six. I enjoy it, but I am a bookies' nightmare in that I don't bet every day, not even every week. I don't have that obsessive trait that makes some people return time after time in search of the thrill that a win gives but in doing so risk racking up losses. And I have to tell you most people are like me, they like a flutter. A bet on the football or playing Super 6 enhances their enjoyment.

A recent Government report into gambling suggested only 0.5 per cent of the UK population were considered problem gamblers – and that figure has not changed since 2012. That suggests that Ray Winstone and I are not doing a very good job! Or more likely that the amount of advertising by the big gambling companies has no impact on the hard core. The gambling addict does not think: there's Jeff or Ray, I must have a bet. They would find a way to gamble come what may. In this day and age with online betting, it is so very easy. I also believe that most people are better off with the household name bookmakers, than doing private shady deals with characters who have unsavoury methods of getting their money back. This is only my opinion. In fact, Ray Winstone and I both spend a great deal of our time asking people not to bet: to use deposit limits, to take time to cool off, to keep track of profit and loss or to exclude yourself completely for six months up to five years. Phil Thompson, Charlie Nicholas , Matt Le Tissier and I did a brilliant advert several years ago where they took the role of three simple tools – it came easily to them – to point out how people could avoid getting into gambling difficulties.

In 2023, I voiced a Sky Bet Safer Gambling campaign, designed to make people think before they bet. It took the form of a trivia quiz with two either/or football questions. For instance, where do Wrexham play their home games? Is it the Racecourse Ground or the City Ground? But question

Yo-ho-no! Not every Sky Bet outfit was a winner
and my look here tells you this was a loser.

three would ask 'What are you betting on?' – the alternative answers were 'Sports I know' or 'Sports I don't know'.
I recorded many variants. 'What are you betting with?'
– 'spare cash or savings?' and 'How do you respond to a
betting loss?' – 'accept it or chase it?' It even asked, 'How do
you bet?' with the alternatives 'openly or secretly?'

I am not naive enough to be saying the gambling companies do not want your money. Of course they do. I can
say they do not want the money of so-called problem
gamblers. They bring with them big fines and bad publicity.
'When the fun stops, stop' has been the slogan for as long

as I can remember. Mind you, half the correspondence I get on betting is from people who are complaining that the big bookmakers will not take their bets or limit the amount that they can put on.

Of course it could have been uncomfortable sitting next to Paul Merson, who has lost a fortune through gambling. But he has taken responsibility for his own actions. I doubt that he would tell you he was lured into it by the big bookmakers. He doesn't lecture me or discourage me and in turn I don't flaunt my £10 accumulator.

I am uncomfortable with slot machines in high street bookies or motorway service stations. I have never, and would never, promote Sky Vegas. I believe gambling should have at least an element of judgement involved. And there are so many online bookmakers these days with new ones springing up all the time that it sometimes appears TV and radio commercial breaks are made up entirely of adverts for Dominos, We Buy Any Car, Go Compare and gambling. I also think there is a case for less advertising around live football. And of course there is an argument that football clubs should not be funded by betting companies. At the start of the 2023–24 season, seven Premier League clubs had betting companies as shirt sponsors with two more having bookmaking sponsors on their shirts sleeves. Top flight clubs could I am sure find replacement backers, but without the money the EFL receives from its sponsorship and individual deals, how many more clubs would go to the wall? Is that a price we are willing to pay?

In my view, though, to ban advertising completely would be wrong. Alcohol is equally if not more addictive, yet we still allow advertising. A blanket ban would mean the end of promoting the Lottery so risking losing some of the funding it provides for good causes.

Where would it stop? Do we stop broadcasting horse racing with its constant betting shows? It must be more appealing for a punter to be able to see the destiny of his money after all. Racing without betting has precious little appeal. Would that kill the racing industry, cost thousands of jobs and be the death-knell for thousands of racehorses?

It is a difficult subject and I completely accept that some people will criticise me for my role. That is their prerogative. Just don't call me a c***!

9

HUNGRY FOR ACTION

Former Shadow Chancellor John McDonnell leaned in towards me. We were in Committee Room 21 at the House of Commons. Somehow I had just spoken at a cross-party meeting on eating disorders.

'Jeff,' he said, 'your speech on *Soccer Saturday* brought more attention to eating disorders than if every MP stripped off and ran around Parliament Square naked!'

A month earlier on *Soccer Saturday*, I had spoken out on the little publicised, little understood epidemic of eating disorders. I hadn't intended to. It was the end of Mental Health Awareness week and the programme was running a feature with Paul Merson and Abigail Davies, who had worked her way up from being a junior at Sky to being a reporter/presenter. They were in discussion with a consultant psychiatrist from the Priory Hospital in Roehampton in London. Merse spoke articulately about the mental health issues he had wrestled with over many years. Abi shockingly revealed that at the height of her own illness, anorexia, she had planned her own funeral. Because the content was so shocking, I had been shown the piece in advance. During the commercial break before it was broadcast, I made a decision to use my platform to speak out. For the ten minutes that the feature ran, I scribbled some words because as a layman on the subject of eating disorders I wanted to make sure I didn't say something stupid. I warned the producer Sam Mills that I wanted to have my say. (She was used to that – I wanted to have my say on everything from the quality of the reporters to the quality of the sandwiches.)

'This is a difficult topic,' I started. 'I have got to be careful to get it right. More people die from eating disorders every year than any other mental illness. The Government's lack of awareness and funding is a national disgrace. They decided to put calories, for goodness sake, on people's menus. The cycle goes like this. Boy, girl, woman, man goes for help. They are told they are not thin enough, not underweight enough to need treatment. They go away and lose more weight. They go further and deeper into the mental morass that they are in. They have suicidal tendencies. Then they are told they are too thin to be treated and are offered palliative care. For god's sake! So we are not going to help you but will try and ensure you die comfortably. It is 2023. Eating disorders are being swept under the carpet. No one should be dying of an eating disorder in 2023. Those with eating disorders need action and help and they need it now.'

I choked up near the end, which at first I found embarrassing. But the response was like nothing I had experienced in forty-five years of broadcasting. The speech went viral.

Social media was awash with people empathising or telling their own stories. People with eating disorders were thanking me for giving them a voice. Abi said she just burst into tears. The *Sunday Times*, the *Athletic* and ITN were among a host of media organisations that wanted to talk about it. Letters arrived at my home. One woman even hand delivered a letter documenting her sixteen-year-old daughter's hospitalisation which involved her being restrained, forcibly tube fed twice daily but included virtually no therapy, no acknowledgement that this is a mental illness.

I told people that the background to this was that one of my closest friends had a teenage daughter who was acutely anorexic. At her worst she weighed just 5 stone 4 lbs (33.5 kg). Her Body Mass Index or BMI was just over thirteen. She was a skeleton. Her mantra was, 'I want to be the thinnest person in the world.' When her parents told her she was killing herself, she told them she would rather die than put on a single pound. She would exchange photographs on social media with others, each trying to prove they were the thinnest. So detached from reality had she become, that it was impossible to have a discussion – every attempt would turn into fearful arguments.

She was not just killing herself, she was destroying her parents too. They would sit outside her bedroom door at night to try and hear her breathing, fearful that she might die in her sleep. As she was eighteen, it was impossible to get her to do anything she didn't want to. A year or so earlier they had managed to take her to the local CAMHS

(Child and Adolescent Mental Health Services). There she was taken into a room away from her parents, weighed against her will, shouted at and given a diet sheet to follow. Needless to say she would never go back. It was the first of many occasions when she was let down by those meant to be helping. When she fell ill with something else, her GP took the chance to examine her and immediately arranged for her to be admitted to the local hospital. Her heart rate was thirty-one beats per minute – lower than many people's when they are asleep – and her vital organs were in danger of shutting down. My friend was relieved though that at last she was in a place where she could be helped. Yet the following day a psychiatrist allowed her home. She had told him that she would definitely start to eat more and that was good enough for him. It is shocking but not altogether surprising that so few in the medical profession know how to deal with this illness. A survey showed that in up to six years of training, medical students spent only two hours learning about eating disorders.

Beside themselves, my friend and his wife rang every private facility they could find to ask for help. Almost everywhere said she was too thin for treatment. Her GP was trying as an absolute last resort to have her sectioned in a final bid to save her, but this might come too late and she could be sent anywhere in the country. At the eleventh hour, the Nightingale Hospital in Marylebone agreed to see her. With the threat of sectioning the only alternative, the daughter told her parents she was willing to go.

Within three hours of seeing the doctor, Helen Murphy, she was in a hospital bed. Dr Murphy was frank about the costs and warned my friends that she did not want them to have to re-mortgage their home. Of course they would have done had they needed to, but luckily they had savings that they would use. They would make a five-hour round trip every day to see their daughter. I went with them more than once. It was a pitiful sight. She was wheelchair bound at first as she had to preserve energy. None of the patients were allowed to walk upstairs but had to use the lift. One of the girls I chatted to a little was being tube fed. She looked little more than a teenager too. It was a heart-breaking scene. Disparagingly, anorexia is known in some quarters as a young, rich girls' illness. That is wrong on every count. There were patients of all ages, from many different backgrounds and nations. I am sure if Rishi Sunak or Keir Starmer or any other politician visited a unit like this, they would be touched and take action.

It was a moving story. Unfortunately it was also a lie. There was no best friend, no best friend's daughter. This was my beautiful daughter Olivia. I wanted to respect her confidentiality as she battled to recover. Now I – and Olivia – want the truth to be told. She was the girl who weighed 5 stone 4lbs and was at death's door. My wife Lizzie and I were the parents who listened outside her bedroom door. Olivia was the girl who somehow grasped a lifeline and held on tight during her eight agonising long weeks in hospital. Olivia still faces a daily struggle to edge towards full recovery,

The war may not be completely won yet, but many battles
have been by my precious, beautiful daughter Olivia.

but her unbelievable willpower means that while the war
is not totally won, she is winning battles. During the cross-
party meeting I was shocked and depressed to learn that
under the current NHS system less than 5 per cent of those
with eating disorders make a full recovery. By contrast I was
encouraged to learn that a scheme in Oxford was claiming
a recovery rate of 70 per cent. I am desperate that Olivia
will be one of those who makes it. I genuinely believe she
will. Since coming out of hospital she passed three A levels
– an A*, A and B – and was accepted at the University of
Manchester. She is starting to live her life and look towards
the future, when once there appeared to be no future.

•

Thankfully, prostate cancer has a higher recovery rate than eating disorders. I completed my thirty-third and last walking marathon in support of Prostate Cancer UK at the start of September 2021. We had raised more than £1.4 million for the charity but, with my knees shot away and my height down at least an inch since the first 'March for Men' in 2016, this was a good time to pack the trainers away. Until September 2023, when I walked my thirty-fourth!

My pal Russ Green and I had set off from Victoria Park, Hartlepool in 2016 to walk ten marathons in ten days finishing at Wembley. (Hartlepool are one of the few clubs never to have played there.) Our aim was to raise awareness of the illness. Many people had no idea what the prostate is or where it is, to the extent of labelling it 'prostrate' cancer. Any fundraising would be incidental in my eyes. There was, in truth, no great altruistic motive behind the marches. A friend of mine Dianne Stradling worked for the charity and had asked if I would be willing to front a publicity campaign. The walking marathons were my suggestion. I had run eight in the past, but after training hard to run another for the Seve Ballesteros Foundation a couple of years earlier, a knee injury had forced me to pull out shortly before the race. I knew my knees would not cope with running. And I am no great shakes on a bike. Actually I am all shakes on a bike – that's the issue. Walking was also something that most people could do. I told people if you can walk to the pub, you can walk a marathon. In truth we had no idea what we had let ourselves in for. Twenty-six gruelling miles later, badly blistered, feet the colour of rare steak and spirits low, we arrived at Marske on the North East coast. In a wonderful moment of humour that lightened a difficult day, a spectator raised a placard that read 'I am Tommy Travelodge!' It was a reference to another daft *Soccer Saturday* catchphrase. Whenever Danny Hylton and Jack Marriott scored on the same day I would say, 'All we need now is a goal from Tommy Travelodge to complete a unique hat-trick!'

At the finish line was a lady who thanked me for saving her husband's life. They had been unaware that he had classic signs of prostate cancer until she saw the 'March of Men' badge that I and the panel wore every Saturday after-noon. She googled to find out more and realised that her man might have an issue. He was checked, found to have advanced prostate cancer, but survived. There was the living motivation for us to carry on. In the years since, people have approached me time and again with similar stories. It was just as well we did have that motivation because during those ten days, everything that could go wrong, did go wrong. We got lost in Leeds and ended up walking thirty-three miles instead of 26.2. On day three, only seventeen miserable souls turned up to walk from Doncaster to Scunthorpe – thank-fully an eighteenth, Lord Ian Botham turned up at halfway to lift our spirits. We ran into Storm Katie. We lowered a walker until his head was just above the waters of the River Trent to rescue the case containing Paul Merson's expensive sun-glasses – only to find they were perched on top of his head. The case was empty. We were chased by an irate farmer as our guides attempted to lead us across his land. We waded through bogs, clambered through waist-high grass, tortured our feet on cobbled pathways. I had tried and failed to sleep in the 'Love Room' in one hotel, the mirrored ceiling offering a most unpleasant sight. By day seven Russ was done. He rang me at 5.30 a.m. to say he could not carry on. But somehow Northampton Town got two physios to his room by 6.30. They patched him up and at halfway in that day's walk, the MK Dons doctor was on hand to check him out.

That was typical of how football threw its weight behind the walks. Not every club though, it has to be said. Manchester United would not let us on their land, not even their car park, even though Denis Law was with us. Arsenal allowed us on the stairs of the Emirates but no further. Others would allow us in the car parks, but not the ground. It was impossible not to compare those clubs with the likes of Millwall, who provided a huge slap-up lunch for everyone at The Den; Aston Villa who opened their ground and lavish dressing rooms to us; Leeds who kept two physios on duty when we arrived much later in the evening than planned at Elland Road; Tottenham who provided us with drink and food and pitchside seating at their magnificent stadium; and little Morecambe who rather than just offer physiotherapy to me and any celebrity walkers, made it available to every single person that day. There were many, many more acts of kindness and support from clubs up and down the country.

Somehow Russ made it to Wembley but we both vowed, never again. Exactly a year later I set off from St James Park,

Exeter heading for St James' Park, Newcastle. It would be fifteen marathons in fifteen days. Paul Merson told me he had looked at a map and it was uphill all the way! Different celebrities joined me each day – the *Soccer Saturday* panel, Kammy, Michelle Owen and Bianca Westwood, Robbie Fowler, Alastair Campbell, Sean Dyche, Andre Marriner, Paul Collingwood, Kevin Sinfield, Colin Murray and many more. Even though there were more days' walking, my body had become accustomed to my daily demands on it and I reached Newcastle, if not with a spring in my step, still with enough in the tank for a night on the Toon. Thankfully this time, a different company, Charity Challenge, had taken

My inspirational friend Lloyd Pinder who suffered
Sunderland AFC and prostate cancer with fortitude.
Tragically, his finishing line came much too soon.

over responsibility for leading the walk and this time there were no wrong turns! They even led me successfully to the pub at the end of the fifteenth day.

Pubs were a hazard on all of the walks. Matt Le Tissier dropped into an inn four miles from the finish line at Forest Green Rovers and wasn't seen again that day. On another occasion, I was caught short and needed to use the facilities at a nearby pub. When I came out of the loo, I found Charlie Nicholas, Kammy and two other walkers taking on board some liquid. The problem was the liquid came in the form of three pints and a glass of white wine.

Two years later, 'Jeff's March to a Million' took in four different countries, Scotland, Northern Ireland, Wales and England. On the steps of Arsenal's Emirates Stadium on the fourth and final day, Prostate Cancer UK's chief executive Angela Culhane announced we had gone through the million pound mark in money raised. But that was not enough. By the time we did our next set of marathons prostate cancer had taken my loyal friend Lloyd Pinder, the former England goalkeeper Ray Clemence and former England cricket captain and Sky colleague Bob Willis. We decided on a four-marathon walk to pay tribute to them. Lloyd had been an avid Sunderland fan so we started in the North East while the second day would take us through his home town in Yorkshire. On day three we marched through Merseyside to finish at Anfield in the shadow of the mural of Ray. And on day four we would visit Stamford Bridge, home of Bob's favourite football team Chelsea en route to the Tottenham

Hotspur Stadium again. The last time we had finished a walk there, Ray and Lloyd had both been there to meet us. Sadly, this time they would both be missing.

Shortly after this I had a falling out with Prostate Cancer UK. They were arranging a 'Quizmas' campaign to be run on Sky. I knew nothing of it until I overheard an agent talking about it. There would be four ex-footballers taking part in a quiz hosted by a Sky celebrity. That celebrity would be Adam Smith. It was my understanding that the former players would be paid a fee for their time. Not to be asked to take part in this was a massive kick in the teeth for me. I wasn't interested in the payment. Over the years of my involvement with the charity, I had never asked for a penny in payment and would never have taken anything. Quite the opposite – on occasional quiz show appearances, PCUK were always my chosen charity for any winnings. I complained loudly, but PCUK insisted the line-up had been determined by the production company in charge of the filming. I said forcefully that they, as the client, were in the position to decide who should appear. It is of course a petty thing in comparison to saving lives, but it made me determined to channel my energy elsewhere. It was definitely thirty-three and out for me.

I relented when Bill Turnbull passed away. Bill and I had started out in broadcasting at virtually the same time in the 1970s, both at independent local radio stations. Our paths quickly diverged, Bill into news, mine into sport but I always admired him from afar. He was a top-class broadcaster, finished six places higher than I would have done in *Strictly Come Dancing* and was a huge Wycombe Wanderers fan. His family asked if Prostate Cancer UK would stage an event and asked if I would be part of it. And so the idea for the thirty-fourth – and final – walking marathon was born.

Kammy, players from Wycombe Wanderers, ex-Crystal Palace and Sheffield Wednesday striker Mark Bright, QPR manager Gareth Ainsworth, former *Soccer Saturday* producer Ian Condron and my son Robbie were among the record turnout of 400. My friend and erstwhile Sky colleague Mark McAdam did a double shift, first reporting on the event then donning his trainers to walk the entire marathon. The irrepressible Kevin Webber was there too nine years after being given two years to live with the illness. The still suave Steve Rider joined in at halfway, where he revealed to me that he had been recently diagnosed. More would have taken part if it was not for the logistical and safety problems such huge numbers would cause. In fact you could say it was 401 participants as one walker carried a life-size cardboard cutout of his dad who had died recently from prostate cancer round the entire 26.2 miles. The walks had come a long way since seventeen or so of us had set off from Doncaster on that rainy day.

The marches are always emotional yet joyous occasions and this was no exception, with Bill's son Will and daughter-in-law Ellie among the walkers. His lovely wife Sesi was at Wembley to wave us off and would be at Adams Park to welcome us there. As we snaked our way cross country, I

Le Tiss leads the way. He rarely moved that quickly
in matches.

listened to the usual stories of life and death, both tragic
and inspirational. Midway through I asked a fellow walker
how he was coping. 'Not well,' he replied and then burst into
tears. He explained how his dad had died during lockdown.
The family had barely been able to see him and couldn't
give him any sort of send-off. For a year my new friend had
been holding in his emotions. Now during the walk it came
flooding out. We talked about his dad's passion for Fulham
football club, how they had gone to watch in the days when
George Best, Rodney Marsh and Bobby Moore had played
together at Craven Cottage and after a while he was smiling
with the wonderful memories.

For every moment of sadness, there was a moment of laughter. One walker was clutching a pint of beer. He planned to drink one every four miles. The only problem was the cans were all in his backpack and were so heavy he looked unlikely to get beyond the eight-mile marker! Almost as bad, he was working at 5.30 the next morning. I wondered which would be the most sore – his feet or his head. We stopped for lunch at Beaconsfield Town FC and sat behind one of the goals to eat. Suddenly, the home club's women's team emerged from the tunnel. There was a match kicking off at 2 o'clock. Instead of the usual sturdy handful of spectators, there were 400 rowdy folk packed into one stand. I can only imagine how intimidated the opposition must have been when they ran out.

We reached Wycombe Wanderers in the early evening to be greeted by hundreds, possibly thousands, of well-wishers. Of all thirty-four marathons, this was by far the biggest welcome and I admit it brought a tear to my eye. Kammy was still going strong and had spent eleven hours solid talking to his fellow walkers. His speech was clear and fluent, even better than it had been in Sri Lanka. He could probably see not just the Adams Park finish line but perhaps the finish line in his battle against apraxia. At least I very much hoped so.

Sesi gave an emotional speech, I yanked off my trainers and revelled in my reward of an ice-cool bottle of Moretti. I was honoured to read Stephen Fry write, 'I and so many others owe Jeff the greatest debt for his selfless work for this wonderous charity. Thanks to his fundraising, Prostate

Cancer UK will be able to fund life-changing research that will benefit so many men and their families and friends. Men like me. And for that I will be forever grateful.' More humbling still was that he called me 'the greatest living Briton'. Well, he is a thespian and prone to hyperbole! The people who truly are great are those fit and unfit, young and old, thin and fat (I fall into the second half of each of those pairings) who put themselves through the wringer to raise funds to beat this illness. This walk raised £350,000 to bring the thirty-four-marathon running, sorry walking, total to £1.8 million.

As if to highlight the importance of continuing the battle, in the weeks immediately preceding Bill's march both Nick Owen and Simon Jordan announced they had prostate cancer. I had worked with Nick many years before at TV-am and he has been a huge part of Luton Town over the years. Luton have been one of those clubs who have always supported the marches. Former Crystal Palace owner Simon, like so many, had no symptoms. He got tested only after a conversation with a friend. When the blood test showed he had the illness, for probably the only time in his life, he didn't argue but accepted that he needed surgery. It is so important that men like Simon and Nick speak publicly about their experiences – just as Bill did and Stephen Fry still does – so that people realise prostate cancer need not be a death sentence.

•

I have tried to use my platform on TV when I can. I don't have the influence of Gary Lineker or the cojones to cope with the amount of stick he takes. But in 2022, I watched a documentary called *The Crossing* following a family of four trying to reach the UK. Mum, dad, son and gorgeous seven-year-old daughter all drowned. I was shocked by some of what I saw on social media and said so. 'Heartbreaking to see desperate people trying to reach England. Some of the comments about this disgust me. I would rather be here with those who want a life in this country than those who shame the human race with their appalling tweets.' I wasn't prepared for the tidal wave of aggressive replies, which to be honest made me wonder what sort of people we have become.

'We don't want the third world here', 'Jeff, you are talking from a pedestal. You don't have to live with droves of economic migrants', 'Sit with the people of Hartlepool who can't afford to heat their homes, Jeff', 'Imagine the trauma of fleeing war-torn France' and of course the inevitable 'Stick to football'. These were among the mildest, most printable responses. We had just watched four human beings die. The producer of the programme actually contacted me to thank me for my support and ask if I would get involved in future projects. I think the only time I have had more abuse on social media was when I said something critical of the then SNP leader Nicola Sturgeon. So ferocious was the response that I half expected to see William Wallace climbing my garden fence brandishing an axe or a claymore! Thankfully many decent people supported my view over *The Crossing*, but it left me pretty depressed about some elements of our society.

As a supporter of a lower league football club which has been on its financial knees more than once, I have also tried to highlight the plight of others when they have run into trouble. Scunthorpe United, Swindon Town and Southend United are among those who have had financial and ownership problems recently and I tried to highlight those issues on the show or on social media. Even if this was only by mentioning their plight, fans appreciated it. Many supporters believe the mainstream media are only interested in the Premier League. Of course, they are, generally speaking, correct. Clubs like the three I mentioned are the heartbeat of their communities, but their difficulties can all too easily be overlooked with so much focus on the top division. Of course, these problems are not life and death. But try telling that to their fans.

10

THE VOICE(S)

When Gary Lineker was suspended briefly from hosting *Match of the Day* by the BBC for comparing the language used in a new Government policy on asylum seekers with 1930s Germany, it was the lead story on news bulletins for days. His team of pundits rallied round and refused to appear in his absence.

I had been told in no uncertain terms that I was not to mention Lineker at all during *Soccer Saturday*. I told Gary Hughes, the head of football, that we would look ridiculous to ignore an issue that everyone was talking about. An hour before the show, he relented. This was no Stelling rant. I simply introduced the show by saying, 'I will have to be at my best today because there is a top-notch football presenter, who is now free on Saturdays!' I had also wanted to warn our pundits that they should be looking over their shoulders with Alan Shearer, Ian Wright, Jermaine Jenas and the rest temporarily at least available, but that was adjudged a step too far! A form of *Match of the Day* was shown, without a presenter or pundits. It was a throwback to how football was televised fifty years ago, offering no insight or expertise. Some people claimed they thought it was preferable. But they were, to be blunt, talking out of their backsides.

People think that what Gary Lineker does is easy. I can assure you it is not. He makes it look easy just as the likes of Des Lynam and Frank Bough did in their day. He achieves that with hard work and in-depth preparation. I was told that before he first hosted the BBC's flagship football show, he would spend month after month doing practice runs in the studio. It certainly wouldn't surprise me. He avoids clichés like the plague. He is witty, insightful and has a great rapport with his team of pundits. With no disrespect to the rest, he is the best. I also admire the way he uses his platform to speak out on perceived injustices. I know he has seen a million social media responses that include the phrase 'Stick to football Gary' but why should he? Why is the opinion of an ex-footballer less valuable than a cab driver's, or a surgeon's, or a twenty-five-year-old MP with no experience of work and precious little of life? (I'm asking for a friend here!)

We are fortunate to have some really capable football presenters in this country. Mark Pougatch is unflappable on ITV. Gabby Logan is versatile and good at pretty much everything she attempts. On Sky's Football League coverage, David Prutton and Michelle Owen have humour as well as insight. They are all nice people too – I guess it is something that just runs in football presenters! Of course, there are many more commentary roles than there used to be as there is so much football on our TV. 'Some people are on the pitch . . . they think it's all over' was Ken Wolstenholme's iconic line at the end of the 1966 World Cup final. But compared to today, he was a man of relatively few words. With no names on shirts, identification rather than interpretation was the key thing then. Hugh Johns, the overlooked ITV commentator that day, would have been focusing on doing the same thing. Barry Davies and John Motson and Brian Moore would eventually take over, followed by Clive Tyldesley and the man we called 'The Voice' at Sky, Martin Tyler. Their role now of course is much more than identification. Every match caller has his own style. The one thing in common is that they will all be immaculately prepared. Some use too many statistics (I know that is rich coming from me) shoe-horning them in at every possible moment as if desperate to use everything they have (I believe that, during *Soccer Saturdays*, at least 90 per cent of the stats I had available never got used). Others approach it differently, like Jonathan Pearce who would paint some beautiful pictures with his words, often describing 'a seagull wheeling away in the distance'. I would look for the bloody thing, but I could never see it.

The best lines are off the cuff, Tyler's 'Aguerrooooo' moment being the obvious example. Or Brian Moore's 'It's up for grabs now' when Arsenal scored against Liverpool in their title decider at Anfield. Motty's 'The Crazy Gang has beaten the Culture Club' as Wimbledon beat Liverpool in the FA Cup final was a little more contrived, but brilliant in its simplicity.

During my lifetime most sports have had a standout commentator whose performances have been right up there with those they are talking about. David Coleman's athletics commentary was so excitable he must have finished as exhausted as the competitors. Harry Carpenter knew boxing inside out. Peter Alliss would say lots by saying very little, introducing humorous little asides at golf majors no matter how tense the situation. Eddie Waring had a wonderful accent for rugby league. Murray Walker's electric Formula One commentary was usually faster than the cars, in contrast to the laconic Aussie Richie Benaud in cricket. Peter O'Sullevan even kept his cool when he described the horse he owned and bred, Attivo, winning the Triumph Hurdle at Cheltenham. He was also responsible for the immortal 'And the mare's beginning to get up . . .' as Dawn Run battled to win the Champion Hurdle in 1986. All these legendary commentators had much in common – they were never bland. They were never patronising. They all added to the events we were watching rather than diminishing them.

But the greatest of all for me was Sid Waddell. I worked on darts with Sid for many years. He never failed to surprise me, to make me smile, to excite me. He was inventive and unorthodox. He had an in-depth knowledge of everything, not just darts. His commentary was frequently laced with historic references. 'William Tell could take an apple off your head, Taylor could take out a processed pea', 'There hasn't been this much excitement since the Romans fed the Christians to the Lions' and 'If we had had Phil Taylor against the

Normans at Hastings, they'd have gone home'. Best of all for me was 'The atmosphere is so tense, if Elvis walked in now with a portion of chips, you could hear the vinegar sizzle on them.' It was apt that he mentioned 'The King' because Sid truly was the King of Commentary in my eyes. David 'Bumble' Lloyd probably came closest to him. Those rich Lancastrian tones enhanced the Sky cricket commentary box for twenty-two years before his career stalled. 'Start the car' would never be heard again. Nor would cricket coverage ever sound quite the same.

I think that it is a mark of the quality of those top football commentators that despite the extra opportunities around these days, no one has been able to stamp themselves as a star of the future. After all, Martin Tyler stayed as Sky Sports' top man until his mid-seventies. That's not to say there are not good people around. I have long liked John Murray on 5 Live and Sky's Ian Crocker is a big personality. I wonder though if in years to come Seb Hutchinson will be the one to make a big breakthrough. Of course it is all subjective. Just look on any social media site discussing the merits of football commentators. Half will think Tyler is the best, some won't. The crazy thing is that so many football fans think all commentators are biased. I am. They aren't.

Nowadays of course we also have co-commentators, sometimes two at a single game, which I believe is one too many! Sky's first was Andy Gray. And he was brilliant at it. As a viewer, he told me things I hadn't spotted, rather than just stating the blindingly obvious. He told me what to look out for before those things had happened. He also had a great voice and a great turn of phrase. His 'Oh, ya beauty, what a hit son, what a hit!' will still send shivers up the spine of every Liverpool fan as Steven Gerrard crashed home a vital goal against Olympiakos. Not bad from an Evertonian! He clearly loved the game. I regard Andy as a trailblazer for everything that followed.

I was sceptical though when Sky turned to died-in-the-wool Manchester United man, Gary Neville, to eventually become their main co-commentator. He had a reputation for being the shop steward at Old Trafford and to outsiders was not exactly a laugh a minute. How wrong I was. From day one, he was unafraid to tell it exactly how he saw it, even though his view might be controversial. He didn't mind taking the mickey out of himself. And he was totally unbiased. I worked with him on the Champions League and a night in Lisbon made me realise how Gary had won over football fans regardless of who they supported. Chelsea had beaten Sporting 1–0 in a group game. Afterwards we headed out to dinner in a popular spot by the river. As we neared our restaurant, a large group of celebrating Chelsea fans spotted him and broke into a chorus of *'Gary Neville, what a wanker, what a wanker . . .'* When Nev waved back at them, they burst into a round of spontaneous applause! Gary ordered his lobster and chips and we were left unbothered. He quickly established himself as the best in the business. And he remains so.

Ally McCoist is good at pretty much everything he does – and that includes co-commentary. He is so relaxed, so good-humoured, so self-deprecating. Though he played the game at a high level, he never talks down to those who haven't. The problem is McCoist, Neville and Gray make it seem so simple that TV executives seem to believe that anyone who played the game can do the job. Robbie Savage illustrated that is not the case in West Ham's European Conference final victory in 2023. 'West Ham are massive!' he yelled as Said Benrahma put them ahead. No Robbie, they are not. A good club, but not massive. There are many worse co-commentators than him but 'Go on Moysey, go on Moysey' wasn't exactly insightful either as the Hammers celebrated their historic win. At least Robbie had the good grace to admit he got carried away with the occasion. And in his defence, he is one of the few who will admit if they have called something wrongly. But I believe his bias when doing Manchester United games is a fundamental flaw. For me, he needs to be impartial (something I think those working on England games should consider as well – they are not cheerleaders). I like Savage as a pundit, but co-commentary is a very different job.

Finding top pundits isn't easy either these days, but I have been lucky to work with plenty. When I meet people there are three questions I am usually asked. 'How is Kammy?' is always the first. 'You look shorter than on TV. How tall are you?' usually isn't long in following. The third is often 'What would your dream *Soccer Saturday* panel be?'

The answer I always give is Matt Le Tissier, Paul Merson, Phil Thompson and Charlie Nicholas. Over my near thirty years of hosting the show, it was the panel I felt had the best chemistry. Of course we have had other outstanding pundits too. Rodney Marsh and Frank McLintock gave a wonderful impression of Statler and Waldorf, the grumpy old men from *The Muppet Show*. Rodney would call Frank 'a dopey defender' to his face. Ex-England captain Alan Mullery was always terrific, Tony Cottee feisty, David Ginola oozed Gallic charm and Clinton Morrison is just a lot of fun. Roy Keane has never been on the show but I would have loved him on the panel – well, I wouldn't dare say otherwise. Sue Smith really gets the show. She has a great sense of fun – which she needs as an Everton fan – and is never worried about gentle digs from the other panellists over her allegiance. I never really worked with Nedum Onouha, but I reckon he has the potential to become a top pundit. And I enjoy listening to the perceptive Pat Nevin on BBC Radio.

Leaving out those who worked regularly on the show, I reckon a panel comprising Graeme Souness, Neil Warnock, Ally McCoist and Jurgen Klopp might make people sit up and listen!

I was going to pick a posthumous panel too, but I suspect Brian Clough, Tommy Docherty, Malcolm Allison and Sir Bobby Robson wouldn't get any further than the first commercial break before the show was taken off air.

It is not easy in this day and age when a misplaced word or an expression deemed offensive to any section of society can cost you your job. It seems everyone is offended by something. I remember poor Charlie Nicholas having to make an on-air apology after he confused Fernando with his Manchester City team-mate Fernandinho. I don't recall anyone having to apologise for mistaking the identities of two white players. By the end of my time I was afraid of saying boo to a goose. The pro-goose lobby might make a complaint.

The Games of My Life

LIVERPOOL 3 v 3 WEST HAM UNITED

AET (Liverpool won 3–1 on penalties)

FA Cup final, Millennium Stadium, Cardiff, 13 May 2006

This game will be forever remembered by football fans as 'The Gerrard Final'. But for me it will always be 'The Wheels on the Bus Final'.

My sons Robbie and Matt were seven and six respectively. They had been to see Premier League games at St Mary's, home of Southampton, just half an hour from my home. But they had never been to a big game and badgered me to take them to one. I managed to get three tickets for the 2006 FA Cup final between Liverpool and West Ham.

Unlike St Mary's, Cardiff was a two and a half hour car journey, a long time to keep two small boys amused, especially in the absence of mum, who would be enjoying an all too rare day without them. Their initial excitement had worn off before we came off the A34 and on to the M4. There was only one thing for it – a sing-along! And so to 'The Wheels on the Bus'.

'The wheels on the bus go round and round,
Round and round,
Round and round,
The wheels on the bus go round and round,
All round the town.
The wipers on the bus go swish, swish, swish . . .'

You get the idea. Our favourite verse was always: 'The baby on the bus goes waah, waah, waah'. Have you any idea how many times you can sing 'The Wheels on the Bus' during a two and a half hour journey? The answer is far too many, even with some of my own unofficial verses added in. The song would be forever etched in my mind.

The Millennium Stadium was a great venue for big games, though the traffic into and away from the ground could be a nightmare, so as we searched for parking I warned the boys that as soon as the game was over, we would race back to the car and make a quick getaway. Their faces fell. 'But Dad, we want to see the trophy lifted. And the team parading the cup round the ground. And the fireworks. Please Dad, please!' I shuddered at the prospect of the crawl home with two very tired children for company. But I defy any dad not to give in to such emotional blackmail. I knew I inevitably would.

We found a nearby pub which was willing to let us in (another first for the boys, though definitely not a last). The brilliant actress Sue Johnston, of *Brookside* and *The Royle Family*, and a big Liverpool fan was holding court in one corner. She made a fuss of the boys, though to be honest they were far more interested in their chicken nuggets and chips.

It gives a whole new perspective to watching football when you also have to give precedence to snacks, fizzy drinks, toilet breaks and explaining who has just done what. And trying to avoid explaining what the word the man next to you has just used means!

But it was worth the effort. The game played on a beautiful day in May was magnificent and Steven Gerrard was even better. 'The footballer on the bus went score, score, score' – and that is pretty much what he did. I can rarely remember a game where the outcome was dictated so much by one player.

West Ham led through a comedy own goal from Jamie Carragher. Jamie had a bit of a reputation for own goals and just couldn't sort his feet out. But he is a brilliant sport – he made one of his first ever Sky appearances as a panel member on *Soccer Saturday* and you could tell he was a natural at the broadcasting game – and that reputation is a bit unfair if you look at how many games he played. Dean Ashton made it two for the Hammers, before Gerrard took over. First a brilliant ball over the top found the easy-to-see Djibril Cisse, unseen by West Ham defenders. Then Gerrard crashed home a volley from inside the box. But Paul

Konchesky's fluke had the bubbles floating into the Cardiff air again and West Ham were almost there.

But just as added time was being announced, in stepped Gerrard again. From our position level with the penalty area at the end Liverpool were attacking, you could see what was going to happen but you couldn't believe it. The ball ran free to Gerrard, who must have been 30 yards out, too far surely. But he struck it low and true beyond Shaka Hislop and into the corner. 3–3! My boys were bog-eyed in disbelief. No demands for fizzy drinks or the toilet. They were as entranced as I was. We should have expected it really. Throughout his career Gerrard was so often the man who produced the big plays at just the right time. The previous season he had saved Liverpool's Champions League bacon with a wonderful goal against Olympiakos and then inspired the greatest of all comebacks in the final in Istanbul against Milan. Years later he would score a wonderful hat-trick in the Merseyside derby. It always staggers me that so many people prefer to dwell on his slip against Chelsea which effectively cost Liverpool their title chance in 2014.

After a scoreless extra-time, the final went to penalties. Gerrard scored in the shootout, as you knew he would, Pepe Reina performed goalkeeping heroics and Liverpool lifted the trophy.

And despite everything that had gone before, this was what my seven and six-year-olds were really waiting for. As Gerrard lifted the trophy above his head, celebratory explosions rang out around the stadium, flumes of blue and red tikka tape were catapulted into the air and two little boys looked on in awe.

Eventually we made it back to the car, parked a long walk away from the ground, especially if your legs are seven and six years old. The crawl out of Cardiff towards the M4 began. Every bus and every car was of course heading in exactly the same direction. We talked about the game, the trophy lift and eventually decided it was time for a burst of 'The Wheels on the Bus'. But the energy plug had been pulled on my lads and before very long the car was quiet. The boys in the car went 'Zzz Zzz Zzz' pretty much all the way home.

They slept well that night as I am sure Steven Gerrard did after his virtuoso display. But as I settled down in bed at the end of an unforgettable family day, once again the wheels on the bus went round and round . . . this time in my head, again and again and again. I couldn't get the bloody song out of my mind no matter how hard I tried!

The Games of My Life

BAYERN MUNICH 1 v 1 CHELSEA
AET (Chelsea won 4–3 on penalties)
Champions League final, Allianz Arena, Munich, 19 May 2012

When Didier Drogba sent Manuel Neuer the wrong
way with Chelsea's fifth penalty, he not only sealed the
fate of Bayern Munich, but also of Tottenham Hotspur
manager Harry Redknapp.

As almost every Englishman in the 65,000 strong
crowd celebrated the most unlikely of Champions
League successes, Harry stood silently alongside me in
the Sky Sports studio at the ground, his face drained
of colour, in disbelief that this was happening to him.
It was still though difficult to believe him when he
insisted club owner Daniel Levy would sack him because
his club would not now be playing in the 2012–13
Champions League.

Chelsea had finished sixth in the Premier League,
five points and two places behind Spurs who had
clinched the final qualifying place for the following
season's Champions League. They would only be denied
that spot if Chelsea could lift European football's most

prestigious trophy in Bayern's own backyard in the heart of Bavaria. As winners, they would replace Spurs as only four English clubs could qualify and the holders automatically had the right to defend their title.

Harry had flown to Munich with his son Jamie who was part of the Sky Sports commentary team. Everybody loved Harry, but he wasn't his usual ebullient self. Leading up to the game, he was a little nervy and edgy, worried that Chelsea might yet deny him the place his side had earned.

It was a miracle that Chelsea had even reached the final. They were a club in turmoil with an interim manager Roberto Di Matteo in charge. The young Portuguese manager Andre Villas-Boas had started the campaign in control. But some dreadful results had put him under pressure going into the last-sixteen game against Napoli. Chelsea had taken only three points from their previous four league games, with a defeat at Everton and draws against Manchester United, Norwich City and Swansea. Rumours were rife that a number of senior players had lost belief in him. At the Chelsea hotel that we were sharing, players were huddled conspiratorially in small whispering groups before they left for the stadium. We had been told that Villas-Boas, who had never played professionally, was going to go into the game without some senior players who he believed had turned against him. He had already publicly said the support of players did not matter to him. Jamie Redknapp spoke to his cousin Frank Lampard, who had confirmed that this was far from a happy group of players. Sure enough when the team was named, Lampard, Michael Essien and Ashley Cole were all on the bench. Captain John Terry was out injured.

The game was at the Sao Paulo Stadium, for me the most intimidating of all grounds. Chelsea supporters, who had been brave enough to travel, were in a cage with a protective mesh above their heads to keep them safe from missiles thrown at them from above. Despite taking an early lead, Chelsea looked like a side that lacked both a plan and any team spirit. Despite the introduction of all the big names who had been left on the bench, they all too predictably wilted and lost 3–1. It could have been worse but for a late goal-line clearance from Ashley Cole. Villas-Boas was sacked before the second leg. With Lampard, Essien and Cole all restored to the team by Roberto Di Matteo and Terry fit again, Chelsea came back to win in extra-time.

A routine quarter-final victory against Benfica followed – not so routine for us though as there was no commentary position available for the away leg at the Estadio da Luz so we sat in the crowd, surrounded by home fans. Thankfully Benfica fans are a lot less aggressive than Napoli supporters. But surely Chelsea would not be able to conquer mighty Barcelona in the semi-finals? Somehow, despite only 20 per cent possession, Chelsea won the first leg at Stamford Bridge

1–0 with Didier Drogba scoring with their only shot on target. The second leg turned out to be an astonishing game of football. By the 43rd minute Chelsea were 2–0 down on the night and had lost both centre-backs. Gary Cahill had been forced off through injury and then John Terry had been sent off for kneeing Alexis Sanchez in the back in an off-the-ball incident. He later called it 'silly'. In our studio, the terminology was a shade stronger.

With no centre-half on the bench, they sent on Jose Bosingwa to play there. This was not much comfort for Chelsea supporters as Bosingwa was in no way a fan favourite and he would be released at the end of the season. Just before half-time Ramires put Chelsea ahead on away goals, but with ten men and only three recognised defenders it was impossible to see them holding out against Messi, Iniesta, Sanchez, Fabregas, Xavi and the rest. But somehow they did. Messi, who had scored sixty-three goals by that point of the season, hit the bar with a penalty and later struck a post. And then, in added time, Fernando Torres, who had such a miserable time at Chelsea, raced clear. Even amidst the deafening noise of 90,000 Catalan fans, he could probably hear Gary Neville's screeching, almost exhorting, cries of 'Torres! . . .' as he rounded Valdes to seal a place in the Champions League final.

And so Harry Redknapp arrived on a sunlit spring day in Germany knowing that his future and his club's

Champions League ambitions were out of his hands. As it turned out, it was like a man turning up to watch his own execution. It was impossible not to feel sorry for him.

I didn't know Harry that well. But he had always been approachable and helpful to me. We had been for two or three meals along with Joe Jordan and some of the Spurs backroom staff before and after European away games. He had also rung me once at home. Now I am not in the habit of being telephoned by Premier League managers. 'Not now Jose, I am walking the dogs.' 'Sorry Pep, the sausages are on the barbeque, I can't talk.' Those sorts of things didn't happen. But here was Harry asking how I was, telling me how much he enjoyed the show until he got to the nub of the matter.

'Jeff, can you have a word with that effing Nigel Spackman and tell him to stop calling me a wheeler-dealer,' said Harry. It was one of the things that really got his goat. And rightly so. In my opinion, Harry was as good as anyone tactically but rarely got the credit for it. I was at the San Siro in 2011 for the Champions League last-sixteen tie when his free-flowing, free-scoring Spurs side was set up in a completely different way against Milan. Despite Harry's public comments that his side would attack, Stephen Pienaar was drafted in for the more forward thinking Niko Kranjcar. Holding midfielders Palacios and Sandro both started too with Luca Modric sitting on the bench for the first hour.

It was not what Milan had expected and when Peter Crouch scored late in the match for Spurs to win 1 0, the plan had worked to perfection. By the way, Harry showed he had lost none of his tactical nous when in *I'm a Celebrity . . . Get Me Out of Here* he volunteered to clean out the dunnies, thereby guaranteeing the public would love him – which they would have done anyway.

I had spent the day of the 2012 final away from most of the rest of the team, just wanting some space. I found it at the English Garden in the heart of Munich. It's a space bigger than Central Park and caters for joggers, surfers – and nudists! It was a glorious spring day so all three were out in their numbers.

There was nothing to concern Harry too much for most of the final at the Allianz. With John Terry suspended after his red card at the Nou Camp, Chelsea had drafted in young Ryan Bertrand. He would make his full debut in a Champions League final. With Arjen Robben playing against his old club and Franck Ribery causing havoc down the wings, Chelsea were content to defend deep, rarely threatening the Bayern defence. The home fans knew it was just a matter of time. After all, they had been imperious on their own ground, scoring four or more goals eight times at home that season. And when Thomas Muller put them in front with ten minutes left, that looked to be that.

In the Sky Sports studio, we felt it was very disappointing to see the English side lose without seeming to give it a real go. It looked as if they were willing to accept a narrow defeat. It was reported that red and white ribbons were already attached to the trophy in anticipation of the inevitable Bayern victory. Then in the 88th minute, Chelsea won their only corner of the contest. Juan Mata swept it in and Didier Drogba, who had been starved of the ball, headed home. To my right, 20,000 Chelsea fans celebrated. To my left, Harry looked crestfallen. Petr Cech saved a penalty in extra-time to take the match to a penalty shootout, where he would go the right way every time and save two more. And then up stepped Drogba to win the Champions League, clinch a place in the following season's competition and send Spurs hurtling into the Europa League.

It was hard to know what to say to Harry, whose misery was not yet complete. He had to stay and watch a fully kitted out John Terry lift the trophy. Then, because of the position of the Sky Studio, he had to walk along the touchline in front of thousands of baying Chelsea supporters who showed no mercy, to reach the exit. At dinner the Spurs boss was inconsolable, convinced that Levy would sack him. Jamie tried his best to get his dad to snap out of his dark mood. We flew home in a private jet the following day and it was the same story. One of football's brightest, sparkiest, most engaging managers was in total despair. He could not accept our reassurances that after finishing fourth and being denied a Champions League spot by the cruellest of quirks of fate, his job at Tottenham would be safe.

On 13 June, less than a month later, Harry Redknapp was sacked. Ironically, he would be replaced by Andre Villas-Boas. Spurs finished fifth the following season and missed out on a place in the Champions League. Villas-Boas kept his job.

11

A DAY IN THE LIFE OF
SOCCER SATURDAY

Football is rarely predictable. In 2012 on the final day of the season, Man United fans were already celebrating winning the Premier League title at Sunderland when Edin Dzeko and Sergio Aguerooooo changed the destiny of the trophy in the dying seconds of Man City against QPR. You never know what twists or turns are just a moment of magic or a referee's whistle away – which is why *Soccer Saturday* was so much fun for years and never, ever predictable as fans waited for the disembodied shout that could change their day, weekend or even season.

There is no standard day but some things are predictable. A typical *Soccer Saturday* schedule went like this:

12.30 a.m. – The editorial meeting which had been running for a couple of hours at the Novotel Brentford bar with the pundits ends. The staff were brilliant and would have happily kept the bar open all night but we were far too professional for that to happen . . . often. We would discuss the footballing stories of the week as well as estimating what time Kammy would show up after a liquid lunch. Thommo loved to predict how many sour-cream coated nachos I would spill on to myself. In fairness, over the years we were joined by the likes of David Moyes, Sam Allardyce, Dean Smith, Delia Smith and a host of other football people which helped with insights into their clubs. It also helped to create the friendships that built the rapport that was hopefully evident on screen.

9 a.m. – Arrive at Sky Sports' high tech site in Isleworth. When I first started to work there, the offices were old wooden huts and the studios were Portakabins. Now there are state of the art buildings, restaurants, a supermarket, a cinema, a car wash and a gym. Generally only a handful of people would be in the open plan third floor of Sky Studios by this time.

9.30 a.m. – In the past my first task would be to go through the sports pages of all the morning newspapers, but Sky no longer provide these, presumably to cut costs. Instead, I speak to our brilliant stats guru Trevor Simmons who would provide me with packs of facts and figures relating to every team from the Premier League to League Two. I had to fend for myself when it came to Scotland or the National League. I had already done handwritten stats during the course of the week, so would only need to make minor adjustments. Then I would stuff them in my briefcase, ready to use them as a starting point the following week. Over the years, I had developed an almost unhealthy fascination for knowing things like how many clean sheets Man United had kept in the season (seventeen in 2022–23), how many goals Stockport County's Paddy Madden had scored since Boxing Day (one), how many consecutive games Kevin van Veen of Motherwell had scored in (eleven – scoring fourteen goals in them). Each week I would spend hour upon hour updating my own stats – and I loved it. I remember spotting Josh McEachran, once of Chelsea, hadn't scored a league goal in almost one hundred games – a lot for a midfielder. Every week I religiously updated that total – 101, 102, 120, 130, 140 – knowing that one day when he did finally score I would be able to blurt out this staggering (to me anyway) fact that few people could know. To hell with updating the Man City or Liverpool score, when Josh did score, this would take priority. Then one Tuesday night, I was sitting at home watching Julian Warren present a *Soccer Special* when the vidiprinter spluttered out, Brentford 1 (McEachran 42) Birmingham City 0. He had scored at the 189th time of asking and I wasn't in the bloody studio! All I could do was shout 'bastard, bastard, bastard' at the TV much to my wife's surprise.

10 a.m. – A good time to go through any scripts and timings with director's assistant Marianne McCarthy to make sure we can squeeze in everything that we need to talk about as well as hitting commercial breaks and opt-outs. If there had

been a Friday night game I would ask an assistant producer for certain incidents to be edited so we could include them in our discussions. During the course of the week, I would log anything I thought was interesting so that our analysis was more than just seeing goals.

10.15 a.m. – Michael Dawson and Kris Boyd ring in their breakfast orders. (Once a pampered footballer, always a pampered footballer.)

10.30 a.m. – The panel start to trickle in to discuss essential matters. In the case of Daws, Boydy and Clinton Morrison this would usually be about who would be next to go out of *Love Island* or which couple was least suited in *Married at First Sight*!

11.15 a.m. – The boys would be suited and booted (or in its present incarnation, sweat shirted and jeaned to appeal more to the nation's yoof) so I would head for the communal men's dressing room. I had been miffed that when the location of those dressing rooms had been changed, my original locker disappeared. On it had been a message written in black indelible ink which read 'To the World's Greatest Presenter from the World's Greatest Darts Player, Phil Taylor'. Phil had written it without my knowledge when he was a guest on *Soccer AM*.

11.30 a.m. – Make-up.

11.31 a.m. – Leave Make-up – I never needed much! Thommo usually took longest.

11.45 a.m. – Into the studio, make sure I have the right chair (it was higher than the others), earpiece in, order soup and a BLT from the floor manager and wait for noon. As may have been obvious, we never rehearsed.

12.00 p.m. – After an opening montage and introductions, we were off and running. Until recently this would involve running through every Premier League game and discussing both teams. In the last couple of seasons instead, we would pick out two or three of the big stories of the week and discuss them. I would research like crazy to try and find different angles, scouring local newspapers and fan sites. It was key for me that we did not just churn out things that had been on Sky Sports News. It needed to be fresh, vibrant and hopefully a little controversial. Of course, it wasn't always possible. It was at times like these that you hoped Paul Merson would produce a gem. He usually did. He is an interviewer's dream. There is no sitting on the fence. He tells it how he sees it. Of course he is not always right. 'Haaland would not score sixty goals in League Two,' he once predicted. 'Man United should have signed Conor Coady,' and 'I think Arsenal will slaughter Spurs, they will rip them to shreds'. It finished 2–2.

12.30 p.m. – If we had any live interviews they would usually be around this time. Managers like Steve Bruce and Dean Smith would often agree to do this. Others were more reluctant. Sir Alex Ferguson did agree to a live spot after he was named the LMA Manager of the Month. Sir Alex was a great supporter of the LMA and wanted to help promote their award. As mentioned back in chapter five, all went well until the PA system sprang to life, then the water sprinklers made him take evasive action and a TV coup threatened to turn into TV carnage. We ended it quickly. Under duress, Jose Mourinho also agreed to a live interview once. He had apparently been told that if he did not fulfil his contractual obligations, the Premier League would take action against him. *Soccer Saturday* was his least-worst option, or so it seemed. On a monitor I could see him taking his seat with a scowl on his face. When the interview started, every answer was monosyllabic. He was like a petulant schoolboy. I knew we had eight minutes with him and I was determined to keep him there for the full duration. I asked around twenty questions in that time. During these interviews the panel often joined in with their questions. This time no one did. Just once Jose almost smiled, then caught himself and the pet lip returned.

12.30–2.15 p.m. – Updates from the big early games. Crystal Palace v Sheffield United, Ross County v St Johnstone and Aston Villa Women against Bristol City Women.

2.00 p.m. – Platitude time. Or rather on-the-day manager interview time. You are more likely to hear someone say something interesting on *Big Brother*. Ok, that could be an exaggeration. The interviewers are only allowed three questions and they all have to be about that afternoon's game. If a manager had run off with the captain's wife, we would not have been allowed to ask about it!

3.00 p.m. – Off and running. This is what it is all about. I always tried not to get too carried away too soon, though when something happens like Phillip Billing of Bournemouth scoring in nine seconds against Arsenal that plan can go out of the window. It is also a good time to announce kick-offs that have been delayed due to motorway congestion, turnstile failure or in the case of one non-league game because the referee could not find a car parking space!

3.05 p.m. – Hartlepool fall behind and my mood gets worse.

3.06 p.m. – Watford fall behind and Elton John's mood gets worse. It was him that pointed out the trend that whenever my team goes behind, his follows soon after. I jot down every goal and scorer as they come through. Initially it is quite easy to read my writing, but as the afternoon goes on, it is increasingly as indecipherable as a GP's prescription.

3.15 p.m. – Charlie Nicholas does his best Mel Gibson *Braveheart* imitation as he bellows from the far end of the studio that someone has gone close in his game. I interrupt everything and everyone to go to him and switch the monitor in front of me to his match, just in time to see a shot has almost hit the corner flag. I know we want the panel to get excited but this is a step too far. The monitor in question means I can switch between around ten games, so as soon as someone shouts, I switch and at worst catch a replay of the incident. The vidiprinter is on another monitor in front of me and on a third is the sports wire service which carries all the big stories of the day. My mobile phone is permanently on the Hartlepool United Twitter (or X) feed. Down my earpiece, I can hear the director, producer, director's assistant and Trev the statistician. This is on top of trying to keep tabs on what the panel are spouting or any reporter may be saying. No wonder I have dodgy ears!

3.50 p.m. – Time for me to run through the half-time scores. The panel's dwindling food supplies have now been restored and Merse usually uses this time to open and rustle a packet of salt and vinegar crisps or Monster Munch and loudly crunch his way through them.

3.55 p.m. – Sky's answer to James Alexander Gordon, Alan Lambourn, will report for duty ready to deliver the full-times in the mellifluous rising and falling tones that only sports results readers are born with.

4.30 p.m. – Time to change gear in presentation terms. Often I would just tell the director to 'Follow Me' – not easy as I didn't know where I was going next. Forget the dull goalless games, I wanted to be where there was a goal, a miss, a penalty, a red card. I would cut across people who went on for too long. Goals would appear on the vidiprinter at machine gun pace. I always tried to mention them all. If you support a lower league side, you want to hear your team's goal called out. The studio shouts are reaching a crescendo as games head towards often dramatic conclusions. It's a horse race entering the final furlong, a 5,000 metres in the home straight. I could never ever get enough of this part of the show. I hated it when the producer would ask me to cut to boring shots of players shaking hands once their match had finished. Stay with the action, stay with the action, I would insist. I physically screamed once when told we had to go for a pre-recorded promo for the 5.30 kick-off when games were still going on. Then having reached the top of the results mountain, it is done. This was like climbing Kilimanjaro to the peak but then having to go back down. The adrenalin vanished with the last final whistle, just as it did on reaching the summit. 'Time for a classified check with Alan Lambourn' was such a deflating phrase (sorry Alan).

5.00 p.m. – Classified results read by Alan Lambourn. A pee break for me. This could be tricky in the past if there was a queue for the nearest gents as I had to be back in position for the league tables. But in recent years Sky's toilets have become gender neutral, which was a result.

5.10 p.m. – Interviews with managers and chats with the panel as the programme meandered towards its close. From 5.30 we would have one eye on the late game. Charlie would often be busy readying himself to dash to Heathrow on the back of a motorbike so he could catch a flight home to Glasgow. The rest of the gang would drift away by car, plane or train, knowing we would do it all again the following week. Until we didn't.

6.15 p.m. – Driving home with the live match commentary on talkSPORT on the radio. I drove myself from the time when a chauffeur fell asleep at the wheel when we were coming back from Cardiff City against Swansea. I would have thought it impossible to nod off after the fury of that derby. You were more likely to have nightmares. I would usually call my wife and ask that we cancel whatever we had planned that night. All I wanted was a beer, a glass of wine and some mindless TV (that's right, *Ant and Dec's Saturday Night Takeaway*) until *Match of the Day*. I would be exhausted. Then I thought of my dad pushing his bike home after a shift at the steelworks and I was a little ashamed.

12

CHANGING MY MIND (AGAIN)

Indecision has played a major part in my career path. At least I think it has.

I left the North East in 1981, a year later than I had originally planned. I had successfully applied for a reporter's job at LBC/IRN, but I changed my mind and decided to stay at Radio Tees. After all, I was just in the process of buying a house overlooking a golf course with upstairs and downstairs toilets costing a whopping £28,000! A year later they offered me the job again and my wife and I took the plunge. We had never moved into the two-loo house – I had changed my mind over that as well. But it was still a culture shock when for a fortnight or so that summer we moved into a Paddington hotel. It was significantly less salubrious than the London hotel where we had spent our honeymoon. The room was so small that the door wedged against the bed every time you opened it. Still, at least it was in a nice part of the city judging by the large number of unaccompanied young, and not so young ladies, who strolled the streets outside late at night.

We eventually moved into a small ground floor flat in the North End Road in West Kensington. Naively we had thought Kensington was posh! We learned quickly that it wasn't – or at least this bit wasn't. It was here I learned that the streets of London were paved, not with gold, but with McDonald's wrappers and discarded market cabbage leaves. I hated it. I had left my home, my friends, the football team I supported and the football team I played for. I was lonely and unhappy in my job. Even the big city attractions – the cinema, the theatre, the restaurants – teased and tormented us as living costs were so much higher than we were used to. We couldn't afford to go anywhere. We used to count our change to see if we could afford a burger the night before pay day. We would drive back to the North East whenever we had the petrol money and whenever my temperamental red Fiat X1/9 would allow. (If the forecast was wet, we would cover the engine with a blanket under the bonnet, hopefully remembering what we had done before I turned the ignition key the next morning.) I hadn't had the warmest on-air reception either. Inside the first few weeks, a listener wrote to my boss Mike Lewis complaining about my accent. Mike defended me, telling the letter-writer that regional accents should be encouraged. The correspondent was determined to have the last word. 'Regional accents should be encouraged, but speech defects should not', he concluded. Another letter was simply addressed to 'Jeff Stelling – Shit'. It didn't even have a stamp but reached me faster than first class mail. I was making my mark, though not in the way I would have wished.

Years later some people would still find my Hartlepool accent unacceptable. I was by now presenting an embryonic *Soccer Saturday* but I was also doing some freelance shifts at talkSPORT. One afternoon, the man who employed me, Neil Henderson, was taken aside by the boss, the legendary former *Sun* editor Kelvin McKenzie. 'For fuck's sake, what is it about you hiring Scots and Northerners? This guy Jeff is too fucking northern – get him off. Where did you get him from? Hospital Radio Bradford?' On and on went the rant. Neil tried to argue my corner but McKenzie was having none of it. 'Get fucking hospital radio Jeffrey off the air!' Years later I was told not to worry. I was no special case. Kelvin hated everyone.

He certainly had the habit of letting the red mist descend. It was rumoured that he fired Simon Stainrod, the former QPR and Aston Villa player halfway through a phone-in. When he wanted to get rid of astrologer Jonathan Cainer, Kelvin said, 'As you may have already predicted Jonathan, we are letting you go.' Neil kept the bad news from me in case my feelings were hurt, but the truth is I wasn't too concerned about the judgement of a man who during his days in charge of the ill-fated Live TV came up with innovations like 'Topless Darts' and 'News Bunny' – a man dressed as a rabbit who gave news stories a furry thumbs up or down depending on their entertainment value. A couple of weeks later Neil was again summoned by Kelvin. 'I was in Marbella at the weekend watching *Soccer Saturday*,' he said. 'I love that guy presenting it. Can you get him in for a chat?' I always respected his judgement! The chat never happened.

My voice still gets me into trouble – with my wife. As many people recognise me through hearing me speak as from seeing me (my height deceives them). On family holidays, when she doesn't want us to be disturbed by someone recognising my dulcet tones, she frequently tells me to be quiet. I am not convinced that is the only reason.

In those early days in the capital, it was in part the kindness of colleagues that kept me sane. I remember Steve Tongue, broadcaster, journalist and author, inviting us to his home in South East London for Sunday lunch in the first week of my job. But in the main it was the football. As I have mentioned, matchdays were not always sweetness and light, but there were some wonderful players to watch. Glenn Hoddle, Kevin Keegan, Trevor Brooking, Steve Coppell, Ray Wilkins, Brian Robson, Trevor Francis and more. Even now, it is hard for me to believe I would go on to be friends with many of them.

There were some clubs you always wanted to cover because their managers made access to players so easy. Graham Taylor at Watford and Aston Villa was the very best of them. After filing my full-time report, I would knock on the dressing room door to ask for a player to appear live on *Sports Report* and it would usually be Graham that answered.

'Barnes, out of the shower now, BBC Radio want you,' he would shout and soon after they would appear. Others too were a joy. I loved being sent to the Dell when Lawrie McMenemy was in charge as you were always assured of a warm welcome by the genial Geordie. The only snag was the radio position was at the far end of the cramped press-box. Once you were in, you were in – as it was impossible to squeeze past working journalists, even at half-time. You had to have a strong bladder or cross your legs very tightly.

Terry Venables was always a great after-game raconteur too. But after he had spoken with the gathered press ensemble, he would often drift away with a chosen few. Those on the outside – like me – would wonder what they were missing. We usually found out when the next day's newspapers appeared.

Howard Kendall at Everton and Keith Birkenshaw at Spurs were others I found approachable. And I had special access to John Neal, the soft-spoken, ever so slightly dour Welshman and former Middlesbrough boss who had been Chelsea's surprising choice as new manager not too many years after I had moved to London. I'd had a good relationship with John on Teesside and he rang me soon after being appointed. Just like me he had found the move difficult and wanted to hear a familiar, friendly voice. Years later you could add the names of Harry Redknapp, Sam Allardyce, Adie Boothroyd and Nigel Clough to the list of those managers you knew would give you a warm welcome post and pre-match.

Others were a little more tricky. You never knew what you were going to get from Brian Clough. In the right mood, it could be radio gold dust.

I covered other sports while at LBC/IRN. I commentated on the infamous 3,000-metre race at the Los Angeles Olympics where barefoot teenager Zola Budd unwittingly tripped the all-American girl Mary Decker. Decker had been favourite for the gold and blamed Budd who was 'beyond doubt' at fault. I was there again when they met a year later in a re-match which Decker won convincingly. I reported on the amazing four gold medal haul of Carl Lewis and was on first name terms with both Seb Coe and arch rival Steve Ovett. I was sent to interview John McEnroe who was at his brilliant best on court at the time. It was an awkward meeting as he was also at his brattish worst back then and clearly had no empathy with a nervous young radio reporter and proceeded to give the most monosyllabic responses to every question. It was hard to believe he would go on to be such a wonderful charismatic commentator when his playing days were over.

By late 1984, I had followed my boss Mike Lewis to BBC Radio and during my time at the BBC, I was lucky enough to work with some of the great broadcasters. Peter Jones and Bryon Butler were the doyens of football broadcasting. Later Mike Ingham and Alan Green would make a fine team. Max Robertson was the voice of Wimbledon for decades, Peter Bromley was the radio equivalent of Peter O'Sullevan in horse racing. The lovely Renton Laidlaw not only had one of the greatest voices in golf but also presented *Sports Report* for a while. Hopefully, I learned a lot from some of very best in the business. My only regret was not getting to work with my broadcasting hero Des Lynam, who by now had moved on to TV. Meanwhile, waiting in the radio wings were some young upstarts, John Inverdale and Ian Payne. The competition was too fierce for me and I headed for the exit – they do say if you can't stand the heat, get out of the kitchen.

In the early 1990s I started working at Sky and was still there in 2023. But I might have been gone by 1995. CNN called me from Atlanta, Georgia and asked me if I wanted to be their European sports editor. I travelled to the Big Peach, was wined and dined, had negotiated four weeks' holiday instead of the standard two and flew back to England ready to make the move. Even eight hours crushed into the window seat by my neighbouring 20-plus stones American opera singer who was en route to Munich to join the German National Opera did not dampen my enthusiasm. CNN quickly got my work permit application underway and I told Sky I was leaving. David Hill, the Australian head of Sky Sports, was having none of it. 'What sport do you want to do?' he asked. 'Whatever it is, you can do it. Go and tell the golf producer, you are his new presenter!'

I was flattered but the real reason I changed my mind was nothing to do with work. I was by now divorced, and I had been dating the BBC's Helen Rollason for a number of months. We both knew that our relationship could not survive based on being together four weeks a year. Her career was booming in the UK, so there was no question of upping and moving to the States with her young daughter Nikki. I phoned CNN to tell them I had changed my mind.

In 2005, Mark Sharman, who I had worked with at Sky, left to become controller of sport at ITV. He rang me and asked me to be their main presenter. Over clandestine drinks in a pub in the lovely small town of Alresford in Hampshire, he made me an offer I could not refuse. Nor did I. I accepted on the spot. When I handed my resignation to Sky's managing director – and my friend – Vic Wakeling, I explained that it would be impossible for Sky to match the ITV offer. He spent a few minutes impressing on me the reasons why I should stay and then wrote a figure on a piece of paper that he thrust towards me. ITV had been gazumped. I changed my mind. I was staying. The call to Mark Sharman was a difficult one and even though he is one of the good guys, he didn't speak to me for years afterwards. I couldn't blame him. But I had almost trebled my salary, so in truth he could not blame me either!

And of course I changed my mind over leaving Sky in 2022. BBC 5 Live had already offered me a job which I had accepted. But I was committed to a podcast, so again I had to tell them I'd had a change of heart. They were both generous in their understanding of my circumstances.

When I announced on air that I would be leaving Sky in May 2023, my first job offer was e-mailed to me within 20 minutes. It came from GB News. I was flattered of course, but my kids already call me a gammon, so it was an easy decision to decline.

When I did finally part company with Sky, 5 Live again offered me a job which I accepted. But before I had signed a contract, Laura Woods had left talkSPORT and they asked me if I would replace her. I felt desperately badly towards those people at the BBC who had treated me so well. But I knew what I had to do. I e-mailed to say I had changed . . . well, you know the rest.

The Games of My Life

BORUSSIA DORTMUND 4 v 1 REAL MADRID

Champions League semi-final, 1st leg,

Westfalenstadion, Dortmund, 24 April 2013

The Sky Sports presentation team watched Juventus hold Real Madrid to a draw to earn a place in the 2015 Champions League final on a tiny monitor in a groundsman's store room deep in the bowels of the Bernabeu. We had applied too late for accreditation, so though we could do pre-match build up, half-time and full-time from pitchside, during the game that was the best they could offer. It lacked a bit of the usual semi-final atmosphere for us, I have to admit.

On another occasion we sat in the heart of the Portuguese crowd at the Stadium of Light as Chelsea beat Benfica. Again there was no studio available.

In Naples, when Chelsea were again involved, we thanked our lucky stars that we were allowed a pitchside studio as far away as possible from the Napoli Ultras. Their party piece was to lob bottles of urine on to the media.

I had been given the chance to host Sky's coverage of the Champions League following the abrupt departure of Richard Keys and Andy Gray. It meant I had to give up presenting *Countdown* on Channel 4 as it was simply impossible to fit everything in. I had few regrets. *Countdown* was a lovely show. Rachel Riley, Susie Dent and the producer Damien Eadie had become really good friends. Damien by the way is the most unlikely producer of such a gentle mid-afternoon show, often sporting a leather biker's jacket and with a vocabulary dominated by words that will never appear on Rachel's board. He is also an avid Blackpool fan. But the time spent covering the Champions League was one of the most memorable periods of my broadcasting life as we visited a cornucopia of the greatest football stadiums in the world, let alone Europe. And a store room.

The Nou Camp in the heart of vibrant Barcelona – or is it Camp Nou? – with Emperor Messi imperious in front of his adoring Catalan subjects. Berlin's astonishing Olympic Stadium, provoking haunting memories of the 1936 Olympics and Hitler's rise. The Estadio do Dragao, home of Porto, which helped convince me in not much more than 24 hours that Oporto on the River Douro is one of the world's most beautiful but relatively undiscovered cities. The space-age, side-on-tyre-shaped Allianz arena, home of Bayern Munich. These were places that would set the pulse racing.

We froze in the Parken Stadium as Chelsea beat the falling snow and Copenhagen in Denmark. We took the

Eurostar to Paris and strolled through the boulevards to the Parc des Princes as Chelsea this time fell to PSG. And we battled against vertigo as we gazed down the vertical sides of the crumbling but still spectacular Mestalla as Manchester United won there. It was all a lot to take in for a Hartlepool lad who had grown up watching football at the Victoria Park.

There were some grounds that I didn't care for too much. The San Siro in Milan, home of AC and Inter, is unquestionably atmospheric, but I couldn't believe how ugly it was. It reminded me of a concrete multi-storey car park, though even I would argue that it was wrong for Italian Heritage to decide it was of 'no cultural interest'.

The most threatening was unquestionably the Sao Paolo in Naples. The approach to the ground may have been like a scene from *It Started in Naples* with colourful washing hung from every tenement building and pizza places and ice cream parlours on every corner. But this was no place for Clark Gable. And certainly not Sophia Loren. Probably not for me either! Crowds would build up from early in the afternoon, starting fires on the terraces inside the ground, readying themselves for a verbal assault on the opposition and possible physical assault on any opposing supporters who had been brave enough or foolish enough to travel there. The atmosphere was malevolent and everyone was a target. Thank goodness we had Napoli legend Gianfranco Zola with us. He may be shorter than me, but in Naples he is a giant.

But in many ways, the most extraordinary place I have watched a game of football was the Westfalenstadion, home of Borussia Dortmund. Sky covered the first leg of the Champions League semifinal between Dortmund and Real Madrid in 2013. I was blown away by the whole occasion. Outside the ground, pavements were crammed with stalls selling beer, bratwurst and Dortmund shirts. Looking around me, buying all three seemed compulsory. I am sure anyone not wearing yellow and black must have been refused entry because inside absolutely everyone was decked out in Dortmund colours.

The Sky studio was simply an open air wooden platform, held up by scaffolding in the heart of the crowd adjacent to the astonishing Yellow Wall. Even with a reduced capacity on Champions League nights, this was one of the wonders of the footballing world. Yellow and black, as high and wide as you could see.

Graeme Souness was with me and I could tell that even someone who had played in front of crowds at Anfield and Ibrox and as manager of Galatasaray had planted the club flag in the centre circle at the ground of arch rivals Fenerbahce, felt this was special. It was neither intimidating nor threatening but felt more like being a guest at one of the biggest parties the world had ever seen.

And what a party if turned out to be. This was a
Real Madrid side near the peak of its powers. Of course
Cristiano Ronaldo was the brightest star, but they did
boast a galaxy. Luca Modric, Mesut Ozil, Xabi Alonso,
Gonzalo Higuain, Sergio Ramos, Raphael Varane and
Pepe all started. They had Kaka, Benzema and Di Maria
on the bench for goodness sake. And their manager was
none other than serial winner Jose Mourinho.

True, Real had played the Germans twice in the
group stages already that season and had not managed
to beat them, but you felt they would rise to the big
occasion against a side who five years or so before had
been battling against relegation from the Bundesliga –
and would be again a couple of years later.

Of course the home team had their stars too. Ilkay
Gundogan, Mario Goetze, Marco Reus, Matts Hummels
and, above all, Robert Lewandowski all started the
game. But they were also reeling from Bayern Munich's
seemingly cynically-timed announcement twenty-four
hours before the game that Goetze had agreed to join
them the following season.

Dortmund's short-haired, soberly suited, heavy-
metal-football-loving young manager Jurgen Klopp
appealed for the home fans to get behind him. But even
if they felt animosity towards Goetze, that was forgotten
within eight minutes as he sent in a curling deep
cross. Lewandowski pulled off Pepe to prod home. The
Westfalenstadion erupted and I remember our platform

wobbling as if being hit by a small earthquake, around force four on the Richter Scale. It would be force five within an hour.

Ronaldo equalised just before half-time before the Pole took over in the second half. He poached a second after 50 minutes, produced a lovely drag back five minutes later before crashing the third into the roof of the net and then scored his and his team's fourth from the penalty spot after 66 minutes. As 66,000 fans went crazy and Souey and I clung to the scaffolding of our precarious perch, Real's players looked shell-shocked, Madrid millionaires bankrupt of ideas.

Lewandowski went close on a couple more occasions and I remember thinking I had never seen such a complete centre-forward performance. He had made history by becoming the first player to score a hat-trick – let alone four – against Real Madrid in the Champions League. Jose Mourinho had suffered his biggest ever defeat in the competition in more than a century of games. Later, even he would admit 'Dortmund were the better side by far'. I wasn't alone in falling in love with Dortmund that night. The following season an average of 1,000 English fans attended each of their home Bundesliga games.

Real went on to win the return leg 2–0 but that wasn't enough to stop Klopp and his team reaching the first ever all-German final against Bayern Munich at Wembley, which ended in a narrow 2–1 defeat.

But as Souey and I joined up with the rest of the team and headed for a local restaurant, where as he would say we could 'put Uncle Rupert's credit card to good use', we both knew we had witnessed something neither of us would ever forget.

The Games of My Life

AMANI CHILDREN'S HOME 4 v 3 ENGLAND XI
Moshi, Tanzania, 16 June 2013

First the excuses. Most of the England XI had never played for England.

In fact the only one who had was Colin Cooper, the former Nottingham Forest, Middlesbrough and Millwall defender who had won two caps. Craig Hignett had played at the highest level for Liverpool but never for his country. Added to that, all of us had spent the previous week ascending and descending Mount Kilimanjaro, the highest peak in Africa. And the night before the game, most of our group had been on an extended night out which appeared to have included an African version of the 'Dentist's Chair' in a local nightclub. (Of course, I hadn't gone as I knew the match was the following day and it would be unprofessional. Plus I had headed straight to the bar when we got back to our hotel base after seven alcohol-free days on the mountain, though to be honest I was so tired I could hardly lift a pint.)

The trip to Tanzania had been to raise money for the Finlay Cooper Fund. Finlay was Colin's son and had tragically choked to death on a screw from a child's toy chair in 2002. He was just two years old. I didn't really know anyone in our party. But I was asked to take part as Colin wanted someone with a little profile to help get publicity and in turn raise funds. Little did I know that by the time we set off on our adventure, Colin would have been named the Hartlepool United manager with Craig as his assistant. If the chairman had seen what happened in this game he might have had second thoughts about the appointments!

Our group – including at least one who was in his seventies – had completed Kilimanjaro's Machame Route, or Whisky Route as it is also known, climbing through the night to reach Uhuru Peak, 5,895 metres above sea-level. It had been exhausting, with long climbs at altitude usually after bitterly cold, sleepless nights in tents pitched on rocky campsites. Almost as challenging was getting contact lenses into my eyes by torchlight every morning with only a bowlful of lukewarm water of dubious cleanliness to wash my hands before attempting it. At least we had portable toilets rather than having to use the hole in the ground long-drops dotted at regular intervals along the route and easily found by following your nose. When I say our loos were portable, they were in the sense that two of the Rifiki, or helpers, carried them up the mountain for us. There was a feeling of real exhilaration when we reached the snow-peaked summit on a glorious clear-skied morning on 13 June. Every single one of our *Dad's Army* style group had made it and it really did feel like looking out from the top of the world. Even better, we managed to raise more than £100,000 for the fund.

I had also learnt that *Soccer Saturday* was popular in the most unlikely places. Halfway up Kilimanjaro, one of the Rifiki, Samuel, had approached me quite shyly and asked for his photo to be taken with me. His friend apparently owned one of the biggest satellite dishes in Tanzania and they could receive Sky Sports. He and his mates regularly watched the show. It's the first and only time I have been asked for a selfie halfway up an African mountain. I am not sure whether Sky's investigation units tracking illegal viewing have quite reached as far as Moshi yet, though I wouldn't be too surprised!

I found the trek down far more testing than the climb. We had been on an adrenaline high heading up through the clouds to the peak, but going down I think the whole group all felt flat and very much in need of a pick-me-up in the form of copious amounts of Kilimanjaro Premium Lager. There was a communal lunch planned when we got back to the foot of the mountain but after a week covered in grime and sweat, all I wanted was to get clean. Four of us jumped into a taxi and headed back to the hotel. I am ashamed to say I stood in the shower for so long that when the rest of the party arrived back, there was no hot water. As we headed for the bar, another group attempting the climb the next day were being briefed. We exaggerated the challenge to such a degree that half of them were ready to quit there and then. It turned out the leader of the party was the sister of ex-Wolves goalkeeper and *Soccer Saturday* reporter Matt Murray! So after a night of celebrating our achievement, it was with sore heads that we set off to the Amani Children's Home on the final day of our expedition before heading to the airport for our return flight.

Tanzania was wonderfully welcoming. Its people were smiling, warm and helpful. But, though economically its fortunes have improved in recent years, it is still a poor country with many issues. One of those is with street children: kids who had lost parents to HIV/Aids or other illnesses or who had chosen to sleep rough rather than face brutality or abuse at home. The children's home is not an orphanage. A lot of the children there had living, but sadly not loving, parents. It provided a refuge for a handful of those who felt safer on the streets than in their home. To us the dormitories, festooned with posters of the children's favourite English football teams, and metal-framed beds may have seemed basic but it was a safe haven to the kids. They knew it wasn't paradise – one told me there was still bullying at times but it was nothing compared to what he had been through. These were children learning to be children again.

And so it was up to us to provide them with a morale-boosting victory on the football pitch at the rear of the Amani home. It wasn't quite Wembley. There was not a single blade of grass, just a patch of rock-hard ground with potholes and bumps everywhere. It certainly would not take a stud – which wasn't an issue for our opponents as they were all playing in bare feet.

If we thought we would take it easy on our eleven-to fourteen-year-old opposition we were in for a rude awakening. They were everywhere – not surprising as I think I counted thirteen players on the pitch for them at one time. They had clearly never heard of Polay-Polay ('slowly, slowly' in Swahili) as they swarmed over us. I was useless. I lost the ball more times than Bruno Fernandes when Manchester United were at Newcastle (well, almost as many). I didn't dare tackle in case I hurt my barefooted opponents! We hoped they might tire but these were East Africans so that seemed unlikely.

With minutes to go we had levelled at 3–3. What a relief, an honourable draw, no loss of face for either side! As we were congratulating ourselves, they raced to the other end and scored again.

Of course the result didn't matter. It was just wonderful to see these kids so full of joy and laughter, when their previous existence had been just that – an existence and a pretty unpleasant one at that.

Our final job was to sign the guest book under the hopeful eye of the director of the home. As she looked on we emptied our pockets of every Tanzanian shilling or English pound that we had. And we did it gladly. Despite the defeat.

13

FOR SERVICES TO RANTING

I've always thought that if I was ever to get a gong in the King's Birthday or New Year's Honours, it would be for services to ranting. I do like to have my say when I disagree with something and thankfully Sky always allowed me to do that. And one of my targets was the honours system.

So it was with shock that I took a phone call from the Cabinet Office near the end of 2023. I was outside Kennington Oval tube station with London buses and black cabs roaring past and I couldn't hear the young lady who was trying to speak to me. I asked her to leave a message – whoever she was! She left a voicemail but again, I could not hear a thing. I texted her number and asked if she could send a text if it was really important. It *was* really important. The Cabinet Office had been trying to trace me. I hadn't replied to the e-mails they had sent (presumably to an old address) and this was the last day for me to accept.

'Accept what?' I asked. The MBE with which I was being honoured, she told me. I am not sure who was the most shocked, me or the London Underground worker standing a couple of feet away as I let out a whoop. 'For Services to Sport, Broadcasting and Charity,' explained the very patient, now no doubt slightly deaf lady from the Cabinet Office. I was delighted that charity had been mentioned and accepted straight away.

Two years earlier, in January 2022, first Matt Le Tissier and then Charlie Nicholas questioned why I wasn't included in the latest gong-fest. I interrupted 'No. Stop. New Year's Honours should not go to someone doing their job well and being well paid for it. They should not go to the rich and famous. They should not go to sportsmen and women for simply winning something. They should not go to political cronies. They should go to ordinary people doing extraordinary things in terms of charity, heroism or terrific community work. Those are the people who should get OBEs and MBEs. Not me and certainly not a lot of those people on that list today.' Perhaps my ire had been raised when I saw that Dr Doom and Professor Gloom, Chris Whitty and Patrick Vallance, had both been honoured, presumably for services to doing the Government's bidding, and scaring us all to death during Covid. In the same honours list were Daniel Craig, Bernie Taupin, Laura Kenny and Vanessa Redgrave. Look, I like Bond movies, singalong with Bernie's Elton John songs, watch the cycling at the Olympics and loved Redgrave in *Julia*. I also cheered on Emma Raducanu, first at Wimbledon, then on to victory in the US Open where she won £1.8 million. I have nothing against any of them. But, as far as I can tell, they were all just doing their jobs. Adele was given an MBE in 2013. I mean, hello? David Bowie turned down both a CBE and a knighthood, saying he seriously did not know what they had been for. 'It is not what I spent my life working for,' he said.

I would have been embarrassed if my honour was bestowed just for doing my job and being well paid for it. Thankfully, it was made clear to me that charities were behind my nomination and subsequent honour. Often the targets of my ranting were less likely to hit the national newspaper headlines. *Soccer Saturday* food, for instance. The infamous BLT sandwiches which turned out to lack the B and the T. The soup that was meant to keep us going was often lukewarm and pond coloured, but when it wasn't available we missed it. 'I am not a political animal as you know. No strong views at all,' I started. 'But we left Europe last night and the consequences are being felt already. There is no soup available at Sky Sports today. We are told soup has broken down. How can soup break down? No broth gets my wrath, for goodness sake. What's next? There'll be no tuna and jalapeno wraps available and then Paul Merson really will be lost.' Soup and sandwiches were not the only inanimate objects to get the ranting treatment. When the vidiprinter broke down soon after the start of the opening day of a football season, I was apoplectic. Forget the presenter, the producer, the pundits, the reporters – it is the vidiprinter that is the single most important thing on *Soccer Saturday*. The rare occasions when it broke down were my worst nightmares. Scores would dry to a trickle. The only goals I would know about were in those games where we had a reporter, I would be missing dozens of goals and was impotent to do anything about it. Or was I? During one commercial break after almost 45 minutes without a score ticking through, I asked a technician what tools he had. When we came back from the adverts, I was smashing the vidiprinter with his hammer (well, pretending to anyway). Eventually the machine took its revenge. It restarted and spewed out a hundred scores in a few seconds, making it impossible to take in what had happened and where!

There were annual rants about my least favourite days. Valentine's Day, Mother's Day, Father's Day – all horribly contrived, artificial, money-making celebrations. I hated Halloween too. When we were kids we were told never to take sweets from strangers. Now we encourage them to do just that one day a year. I loathe the false bonhomie of New Year's Eve when we hug and kiss people that we have spent the other 364 days of the year moaning about. At least there is New Year's Day football to look forward to. I always made a point of presenting that show as I knew I would not have been out celebrating until the early hours. Worst of all though is Bonfire Night. Talk about burning money! As an animal owner and lover too, it is impossible to keep them from being terrified. And it seems to go on for weeks. Just in case you think all this makes me sound a shade curmudgeonly, I am not against organised fireworks' displays on the nearest Saturday to 5 November between 7.30 and 9 p.m. That's reasonable, isn't it? Outside of those times I advocate offenders being pinned to a Catherine wheel. I would not want to appear a Grinch. I do love birthdays, Christmas Day and Boxing Day (admittedly for the football).

•

I like to defend my native North East too. It's not perfect, not a Bo Derek '10', but wherever I have lived in England, I have always regarded it as home. My defence of Middlesbrough in 2007 is still shown at events these days – now that is unbelievable, Jeff. It was inspired by a survey carried out for the TV show *Location, Location, Location* which claimed Middlesbrough was the worst place in England to live and Hartlepool twentieth worst. I launched into it. 'To be honest, I thought it was upside down, Look this is not a rant (it definitely was) but the people who compile this tosh, no disrespect, are the type who go north of Rickmansworth only when they go to the Edinburgh Festival Fringe and thinks everyone in the north lives in Coronation Street-style terraces. They are the type who drink skinny lattes and call their mushy peas guacamole.' Of course skinny lattes needs updating today to maple hazel latte or lapsang souchong tea. I will come clean – I drink skinny lattes these days, modern man that I am. And so, egged on by the *Soccer Saturday* gang of four I ran through a list of North East beauty spots and famous names that came from the town, before coming to my conclusion. 'Ok, it's not quite as nice as Hartlepool, but Middlesbrough is a darn good place to live.' One of those famous names was Brian Clough and sometime later the town honoured me with a brass bust of the great man.

That survey was no doubt put together by faceless people at a southern-based agency. But my rant about Newcastle was aimed at talkSPORT's Ian Abrahams, aka 'Moose'. He had told listeners that the reason Newcastle United attracted 52,000 fans to St James' Park every week was because there was nothing else to do in the city. I let him have it with both barrels. 'Now this is not a rant,' I started. 'But he has probably never been to St James' Park, he has probably never had a night out in the Bigg Market. He has probably never eaten at any of the wonderful restaurants. He has never appreciated the marvellous architecture of Grey Street. He will never have been to the Theatre Royal, never have been to the racecourse. He will never have strolled along the Quayside in the shadow of the Tyne Bridge. I doubt he has ever visited the Baltic Gallery. He probably doesn't know that Greggs opened their first ever branch in Newcastle in 1951. He's never had a Newky Brown. And he's never had a stottie cake – actually he probably has eaten a stottie cake, quite a lot of them in truth. It's a wonderful city with loads to do and lots to eat and loads to drink. Don't believe what you hear on the radio, trust me!' I felt a little sorry for Moose, who would later apologise for his comments but not before *The Mag* in Newcastle had run a transcript of my mini-rant under the headline 'Jeff Stelling tears talkSPORT idiot apart.' I was at an event with Ian a few weeks after this and he was reluctant to approach me as he felt he had offended me. But I understand the game. He was trying to provoke a reaction. He was just unlucky that he picked on one of my favourite cities, not just in England but in Europe.

It was ironic that a few years later I would be working alongside Moose at talkSPORT. I would also be in the studio with Gabby Agbonlahor. When Aston Villa beat Southampton 1–0 in a live Sky game, I said, 'It was right up there with the worst ever Premier League games.' I didn't think that was remotely controversial as the Villa captain John McGinn had already admitted he would have turned it off if he had been watching. So I was surprised to read in the Midlands media that Gabby had told me to shut up! The ex-Villa striker wrote, 'Stelling has a lot to say. Shut up man!' I referenced his comments on that Saturday's show but mischievously called him Gary Agbonlahor. It would make for an interesting first meeting when I took up my new job on the breakfast show at talkSPORT.

Rightly or wrongly I have used my platform to defend my region and also my family. When my son Matt picked up a £100 parking fine on his way home from Brighton's game at Manchester United I was livid. He follows the Seagulls home and away and had dropped off a friend who was catching a train home at Crewe Alexandra's ground after the match. He paused to take a gulp of water and set off again without ever moving into a parking bay. Because the entrance to the car park was monitored by automatic number plate recognition, he was deemed to have dodged payment by one of the big private operators. I showed the letter to viewers. 'It is a £100 parking fine for, as it says here, five minutes' parking. That works out at £1,200 an hour. Honestly, this should be against the law. I am not blaming Crewe Alexandra but they should take a look at who they are associated with because it doesn't do their reputation any good at all. £1,200 per hour. Hang your heads in shame.' To their credit, the football club were in touch before the end of the show, to tell me they would get the fine rescinded and they did. I was speaking at a dinner there a few months later and the first thing I did was make sure they provided me with a parking space! It may have seemed a trivial thing – and this is not a rant – but parking fines in this country are shameful. Private companies issue more than 20,000 tickets a day, some justifiably but many – as in my son's case – with no justification. Thank goodness there has been a clampdown recently on them, no pun intended.

Sometimes during *Soccer Saturday* the football got in the way of the ranting of course, but at least now I am Little Gobshite, MBE!

14

HARTLEPOOL GOES TO HOLLYWOOD (ALMOST)

My telephone call with two Hollywood actors in the summer of 2020 was potentially the most important discussion in the history of my struggling football club, Hartlepool United. It was an opportunity to not only secure its future but also to make it a household name across the world.

For several weeks I had been talking to Steve Horowitz from Inner Circle Sports, a New York based company whose speciality was facilitating sporting takeovers or investments. Their portfolio included involvement with the likes of Inter Milan, Crystal Palace, Sunderland, Barnsley, Portsmouth and most famously Fenway Sports Group, owners of Liverpool. The company has also advised on the sales of teams in the MLS as well as baseball, American football, basketball, lacrosse and a host of other sports. They were unquestionably the real deal. I had been introduced by Shaun Harvey, the former EFL chief executive, who told me there might be some interest in buying Hartlepool United.

I e-mailed Steve to introduce myself, explain a little about the football club and attached some photos of our fans in the fancy dress outfits that they wear in their droves for the final away game of the season. Over the years, our fans have travelled to the last match as Thunderbirds, Morris Dancers, Oompa Loompas, Where's Wallys, Smurfs, mime artists, clowns, Star Wars Stormtroopers, medics and perhaps best of all, they travelled to Crawley as penguins. The astonished looks on the faces of Londoners and tourists alike as hundreds of giant penguins used the escalators at underground stations was a sight to behold. I thought the photos might catch Steve's attention. As it happened he e-mailed back, to say he knew just who I was. 'Appreciate the introduction, but your reputation precedes you, even for an American like me!' he wrote. He had also been speaking to Ian Scobbie, a solicitor, who had once worked with Pools and who I knew well. Ian and I together had negotiated the lucrative naming rights deal with Sky Bet which resulted in Victoria Park becoming the 'Super Six' stadium for a little while. He told both of us that the proposal he was dealing with was a little different than the norm, but he could say no more at that stage. I remember him asking how much we believed the chairman, Raj Singh, would want for the club. I felt that a figure of around £500,000 would be enough to at least kick-start a conversation.

Raj had stepped in to save Hartlepool United when no one else would. The previous owner John Blackledge had lost around £2 million in eighteen months – a staggering amount. I felt for him as he had, generally speaking, left the club to be run by people he trusted and they let him down very badly. He made it clear that he would not spend a penny more. Pools were left facing a winding up order with HMRC chasing nearly £200,000. Administration and ultimately liquidation looked certain. The home game on 20 January 2018 looked set to be the last. It was a sell-out. Fans from neighbouring Middlesbrough came in their hundreds. They remembered how their club had faced expulsion from the Football League if they failed to play their opening game of the 1986–87 season. With Ayresome Park padlocked, Hartlepool stepped in to allow the match to take place at Victoria Park and give Steve Gibson the breathing space to complete his takeover. At the game itself, opposing supporters threw £10 and £20 notes into collection buckets. The opposing supporters were from Wrexham.

Pools staggered on. They took loans from the local council to pay players' delayed wages. A young fan, Rachel Cartwright, had set up a Just Giving page which raised an astonishing £84,000 to try and stave off what seemed to be the inevitable. Home games were under threat due to an inability to pay for policing and St John Ambulance services. Even the chip shop at the ground had been closed as it was too expensive to run. It was not an appealing prospect for any buyer. I had spoken to a number of potential purchasers, from local businessmen to Swedish consortiums. All had fallen through. Raj was the last resort. I had never met him but I – and everyone in the North East – knew he had been chairman of arch rivals Darlington and they had gone into administration, despite him putting in a significant amount of money.

I went to see Raj at his home with ex-Liverpool and Middlesbrough star, Craig Hignett and a member of the Supporters' Trust. Raj agreed to invest if someone else would at least make a gesture. He pledged £1.2 million over four years. In fact he eventually put in far more than that. My 'gesture' was £100,000. I would need a hell of a good explanation for my wife. Debts were cleared, money was invested into the team and the chip shop was re-opened.

So the club was in decent shape when the American interest came. After a number of exchanges, Horovitz asked me if I would speak with the two potential buyers over the phone. They had five clubs on their radar. They were looking for a club in a working class area, close to the sea and with potential to move up the leagues. They also wanted to support the local community and were initially willing to invest £5 million over three years. Steve told me when I found out the identity of the Hollywood buyers, my mind would be blown. I doubted that as my cinematic heroes tended to come from the John Wayne era. If it was Dustin Hoffman and Tom Cruise then I would have been impressed. But for now the would-be benefactors would have to remain anonymous. Before the conversation started I was told that we were probably third favourites to win the five-horse race. The call to Los Angeles started well. The mystery men had an easy charm and were good listeners as I filled them in on why Hartlepool was the obvious choice. One clearly knew his football, the other less so. We talked about the fans. I told them that one in five of the town's population had travelled to Cardiff in 2005 for a play-off final against Sheffield Wednesday. They had seen the photographs I had sent of supporters in fancy dress and clearly loved that. Then I told them about our nickname and they were entranced (they might tell you bored, but I prefer entranced). I felt the less football orientated of the two was especially interested.

Hartlepudlians are known as 'Monkey Hangers'. The reason dates back to the Napoleonic Wars when a French warship was wrecked on the Longscar Rocks just off the coast. A survivor was washed up on the beach, dressed in military uniform. He was given a summary trial, but when he remained silent, he was declared guilty and hung. He turned out not to be a French spy, but a monkey. He was treated as a pet on board ship and had been put in uniform for the amusement of the crew. Hence the nickname, which for many years was used as a derogatory comment to the people of the town. Even now I get the odd heckler at public events demanding, 'Who hung the monkey?' The stock reply is 'Why? Are you missing a relative?' But the town really embraces the epithet now. One of the local rugby clubs had a hanging monkey on their crest, Pools' mascot became H'angus the Monkey and the council erected a statue of the animal at the town marina.

The call lasted around an hour and a half. Within minutes Steve Horowitz rang me. 'You are now number one,' he told me. They wanted to look at the books and were happy to sign a non disclosure agreement. I was ecstatic, but I knew the next steps could not involve me. This was Raj's club; it was mainly his money and the decision would have to be his. I e-mailed him the next day, outlining what had happened. I told him that, unlike others who had approached us, I believed they were serious players. I pointed out that they were represented by an agency with an outstanding reputation who normally worked at a higher level, and that this could have been an opportunity to secure the future of the football club for years to come, using their money, not his. I told Raj that I thought he had more than done his bit and put in far more than anyone could have expected. If we could have found new investors at that point, he could have walked away with his head held high and forever be seen as the club's saviour. I told him that I had mentioned the fact that he was not desperate to stand down, and I had the impression that they would have been willing to come to some agreement over a payment to him. I relayed that they had made it clear it would not be the amount Raj had put into the club, but it would have meant that rather than continuing paying the bills, he would have had money coming into the club – that had to be a first. I told him that they wanted to move quickly and get a deal done soon for a club. I said that if we missed this opportunity, they would go elsewhere!

How prophetic those words would be. Raj told me he had no problems showing our accounts, but I got the impression he would be happier if he still had some role at the club. I suggested this to Inner Circle and also told them that they now had to deal with him direct.

I had two further calls that I recall from Steve. The first to tell me they had made an offer, but the chairman had rejected it and wanted all of the money he had invested back. This would be in the region of £1.8 million. To my knowledge, this was an accurate valuation of the commitment he had made to the club. He had spent not just his time, but his money, and had more than fulfilled his promises when he first took over the club. They felt this was an opening gambit, but when they made contact again the position was unchanged. If, as is claimed, Wrexham were always their top target, why did the deal broker ring me to tell me definite bids for my club were being made?

I don't remember when Steve Horowitz revealed that the investors were Ryan Reynolds, the star of *Deadpool* and many other top movies, and Rob McElhenney, creator of US sitcom *It's Always Sunny in Philadelphia*. He told me that they were ready to walk away unless the chairman changed his stance. 'Would Raj be starstruck?' he asked. 'If I told him their names, would he change his mind?' He would not and he did not. I believe he felt he had made an investment when the club was at rock bottom. Now under the manager, Dave Challinor, the team was challenging for promotion back to the Football League and the chairman understandably wanted to reap the rewards from the hard work and the money he had put in. Pools were promoted via the play-offs, so Raj did get to enjoy the accolades from the fans, who of course were unaware of the American interest.

•

On 9 February 2021, nine full months after they had approached Hartlepool United, Rob and Ryan – I feel that I can be on first-name terms after our long conversation, even though we still have never met – officially became owners of Wrexham FC, a club in a working class area, by the sea and with potential to move up the leagues. Soon they were paying big money for players. Even former Premier League players were arriving at the Racecourse Ground. A Netflix documentary *Welcome to Wrexham* would make the football team from North Wales famous worldwide. They won promotion back to the Football League – ironically swapping places with Hartlepool who were relegated back to the National League. They travelled to the States to play Chelsea and Manchester United and other top sides in preseason. We played Blyth Spartans and Redcar Athletic. They announced plans to build a new stand and, as promised, they put money into community projects, providing unwell children with much-needed financial aid to help fund operations, buying local teams football kits and helping the locals celebrate victories in style at local pubs. In every respect they were dream owners. They have sprinkled their stardust around the lower divisions. While they had A-lister Hugh Jackman as their guest at a game, Hartlepool had me. I'm not sure I am on any list! I genuinely think their clear and high profile enjoyment of being owners of a lower league club may attract others to do the same.

I kept quiet about the whole sequence of events until Humphrey Ker, the Welsh club's executive director, opened up on why they had been chosen. He insisted Wrexham had been the front runner all along and Hartlepool had been a second front if things went wrong. That may be right, but it is strange that Reynolds and McElhenney were not announced as potential investors at Wrexham until the end of September, three months after they had been talking with me. Humphrey also insisted that one of the criteria where Hartlepool had fallen short was its proximity to Middlesbrough, Sunderland and Newcastle. In truth, Hartlepool is thirty-two miles from Newcastle, Wrexham is twenty-five from Liverpool, which does have a couple of decent teams if I recall. Look, Humphrey is a foot taller than me so I am not going to argue too much. Raj has since spoken about it too. He was always unhappy that he was being asked to deal with two anonymous people. In fairness we had spoken to a lot of potential investors over the years who have turned out be total time wasters. I believed though that the involvement of Inner Circle, whose reputation was matchless, was guarantee enough. I was told later by a very good source that he did not trust me and my part in the negotiations, but everyone knows my only interest was to act in the club's best interests. I would like to think that when he had time to reflect, the chairman would have realised that I stood to gain nothing had the Americans taken control of the club. Ironically, by the summer of 2023, Hartlepool United were up for sale again with the chairman reportedly open to offers of around £500,000. I am not sure how accurate the figure was as I certainly was not getting involved again.

Of course I was gutted, but if it wasn't to be us I was pleased they had chosen Wrexham. I remember the day they were relegated from the Football League. Our reporter at the match that decided their fate was lifelong Wrexham fan Bryn Law. Unable to control his emotions, he wept live on *Soccer Saturday* as he struggled to describe his club's demise. The club went on to suffer administration and fifteen long and frustrating years out of the Football League. Big names like Dean Saunders, Gary Mills and Brian Flynn were among a long list of managers who tried and failed to turn the club around on the field. The hope of a swift early return soon faded and they seemed almost to have accepted that the fifth division was their natural place, before the takeover. I am sure many of their fans, who had also been supportive of us in our darkest hours, must have found it hard to believe. Good luck to them.

Who knows, perhaps in years to come Ryan Reynolds or Rob McElhenney might think 'The Hartlepool Monkey' could make a decent movie!

15

NON-LEAGUE MATTERS

I was watching the replay of a shot and a save on the monitor in the comfort of my directors' box seat. This wasn't though Tottenham Hotspur's swanky new ground or the Emirates Stadium. It wasn't even Selhurst Park, home of Crystal Palace (though I have to admit I do like their heated seats!). I was actually at Hayes Lane, the home of Bromley FC and I was watching them play Hartlepool United in the National League.

I remember when my club was relegated from the Football League for the first time in its inglorious history. I had donned my blue and white shirt at half-time live on Sky Sports during the final-day fixtures in the forlorn hope of a footballing miracle. We needed to beat high-flying Doncaster and hope Newport County failed to beat Notts County. Two second-half goals from Devante Rodney had given us an unlikely lead while the Welshmen were being held by Kevin Nolan's team. But with Newport playing a 1-2-7 system, defender Mark O'Brien scored the 90th-minute goal that sealed our fate. I was devastated. I tried to present the closing minutes of the show reasonably professionally but my heart was broken. This was the end. After all, football did not exist outside the top four divisions. Or so I had thought. But over the next few seasons, I realised that not only does football carry on outside the EFL, but it is just as enjoyable and exciting if, at times, a little more eccentric.

I remember going to Aldershot with my son Robbie. He was doing radio commentary on the game. I was going as a Pools fan (and president of the club). As we arrived at the ground, the heavens opened, rain bouncing inches high off the pavement. I parked and we waited for the biblically proportioned downpour to relent, but there was no sign of that happening. Then I saw a man protected by an umbrella running across the flooded car park towards us with a second umbrella in hand. It turned out to be Shahid Azeem, the Aldershot chairman. Try as I might, I couldn't imagine Daniel Levy or Avram Glazer galloping across the tarmac at Tottenham or Old Trafford to ensure one of the media corps – or even one of the opposing directors – stayed dry.

I had been to Aldershot before and been invited to eat with their directors. But there was no ivory tower boardroom for them. We all ate with hundreds of supporters in a banqueting suite. To be honest, it was all the more enjoyable for it. And the diners made more noise than the fans.

Hartlepool had stolen a 1–0 win at Dagenham and Redbridge in the 2023–24 season thanks to an own goal and a brilliant display by our goalkeeper Pete Jameson. As I headed back to the boardroom, I had to walk through the home supporters' bar, occupied by hundreds of disconsolate fans. As I was spotted, some gentle good-humoured booing began. It continued as I waved theatrically to each corner of the room, before turning into a spontaneous wave of applause. Not for the first time, I thought non-league supporters were the heart and soul of football.

Talking of food at Aldershot, I was lucky enough to try Kidderminster Harriers' pies on a trip to Aggborough. Man United or Arsenal or Liverpool might have had the most expensive players in recent seasons, but non-league Harriers had the most expensive pies. Not only were they pricey, but they were different gravy – the Lionel Messi of pies. They won award after award. As a man who has frequently been accused of eating all the pies, I can safely say they were the best. Sadly the man who made all the pies, Brian Murdoch, passed away and though I have not been back to Kiddy so far since their return to the National League, I suspect things are not quite the same.

I remember visiting Meadow Park, the home of Boreham Wood. This brings to mind the old gag: follow the crowd on matchday and you will end up in Tesco. Their attendance is often below 1,000 and has been known to dip below 400. They survive in part due to the fact that Arsenal Women play most of their games at the ground. If more of their matches are played at the Emirates in future, I suspect that will be good news for women's football and very bad news for Boreham Wood. It does lead to an unusual atmosphere and for me an unusual experience. I was sitting in a half-

My son Robbie and his friend Milo ready for Pools' last away
game of the 2018–19 season. Sadly, Barrow put us to the sword.

empty stand close to the dugout when I made a comment
about the referee. Luke Garrard, the home manager, turned
to me and said something like, 'If you think he is bad, you
should have seen the one we had last game.' The ice was
broken and throughout the rest of the game we continued
a sporadic conversation over decisions, missed chances, the
quality of the two sides, anything really. I almost asked him
where he was going for his summer holidays! I think if I can
get a seat close enough to the dugout at the Etihad, I might
try the same thing with Pep Guardiola.

I certainly wouldn't pretend that every ground in the National League, or the levels below it, has TV monitors for visiting directors. Dorking Wanderers' Meadowbank Stadium has a capacity of less than 2,000. Still, this is an improvement as they used to stage their games on public playing fields. You can forgive them though as they are a remarkable story. Formed in 1999, their players used to pay subs to the club. Eleven promotions later and the club now pays the players. But there are some big clubs outside the EFL and some correspondingly good grounds. Chesterfield were robbed of an FA Cup final appearance in 1997. If VAR had existed then a ball that was clearly over the line would have been given as a goal (depending on who the VAR was!) and Chesterfield would have played Chelsea at Wembley. They may play outside the Football League now, but they play inside a glorious 10,500 capacity stadium which would grace most league clubs.

Oldham are a former Premier League club. Their Boundary Park ground holds more than 13,000. Until recently Notts County, Wrexham and Stockport County, all with proper Football League histories and grounds to match, played in the fifth level of the English game. In 2022, Notts County attracted an astonishing 16,511 to their game with Yeovil, a crowd that Premier Leaguers like Bournemouth or Luton could only dream about. Of course, sod's law, the game finished 0–0!

And don't think you'll be mixing it with the hoi polloi outside of the EFL. In recent seasons I have bumped into former

England cricket captain Michael Vaughan and ex-Liverpool star Didi Hamann at Macclesfield, Gary Pallister and Lee Clarke at Hartlepool, former Arsenal royalty Paul Davis and ex-*EastEnders* star Tom Watt at Barnet. I've sat next to big Mick Harford at Eastleigh as we watched two teams try and play in water so deep that Tom Daley could have safely dived into it and emerged unscathed. Denis Bergkamp has been spotted at Bromley – he may like the TV monitors in the director's area – but it was probably because his son was playing for the London side in the National League.

It is not just a Bergkamp who has performed in the National League either. Michail Antonio, Chris Smalling, Jamie Vardy, Troy Deeney, Glen Murray, Jarrod Bowen, Max Kilman and a host of others have played at that level. In 2023, former England keeper Ben Foster was playing for Wrexham while Richard Stearman, who played in the Premier League at Wolves, was at Solihull Moors. Will Grigg, who was once ranked twenty-fifth best player in Europe, was leading the attack at Chesterfield. *Love Island* star Luke Trotman played for Darlington in the National League North and Tom Clare who was in the same reality show was a striker for Macclesfield, further down the non-league ladder (you can make up your own gags about scoring!). Former England manager Peter Taylor had a spell in charge at Dagenham and Redbridge.

It is not perfect. The gulf between the haves and the have-nots is a chasm which means the playing field is far from level. A couple of seasons ago wealthy Stockport

County amassed ninety-four points while Dover Athletic finished bottom with *one* point from their forty-four games. They actually accrued thirteen points but were docked twelve by the league. What's more, there are too many 3G and 4G surfaces. The game I was watching on the monitor in the Bromley directors' box was being played on an artificial surface. For many clubs these pitches make vital money by being used all year round by the local community. In that sense it is hard to criticise. But if any club that uses a plastic pitch gets promoted to the Football League they have to replace them at huge expense. And clubs at National League level are still only allowed to name five substitutes and use only three, which leads to many teams not having a keeper on the bench. Worst of all, there is still only one automatic promotion place, despite frequent promises that this will change. Protectionism still rules in the EFL.

So while it may not be the Football League and it might barely be given lip service in the media – in fact, it gets so little publicity that fans of so-called big clubs think it is not important – it is still football and it is still fantastic. And my god, it is important to me and hundreds of thousands of others. When Hartlepool managed to lose 5–2 on the artificial surface at newly promoted Oxford City after leading 2–1 at half-time, I received a tweet. 'What was the Hartlepool score today @jeffstelling?' It is the sort of tweet you get all the time from gloating football fans. But this one came from the director of football at Oxford City! It matters alright.

16

THE TOURS

I was reluctant to commit to a theatre tour with the old *Soccer Saturday* panel. The last time we had tried this I ended up £235,000 out of pocket. The promoter had sued Paul Merson and me after the opening two shows in Southampton and Bournemouth. Both had been really well attended. The case never got to court but eighteen long, depressing, worrying months passed before the two sides came to an agreement at a mediation settlement shortly before the first scheduled hearing. No money changed hands. The only people who benefited were barristers and solicitors who appeared to charge by the word, rather than the hour. My £235,000 had gone exclusively to them. Merse had hired a brief who was a dead ringer for Rumpole of the Bailey but in the end, Paul and I came to an agreement with the opposition without a single member of the legal profession in the room.

But with a different promoter, Michael McPherson, nephew of Eric 'Monster' Hall, we agreed to do it again. Ironically our first night was again at the Mayflower Theatre in Southampton. Thanks in part to the attraction of Matt Le Tissier, the place was a 2,300 sell-out. My role was to ask questions, weigh in with the occasional story and open the show with an extended ten-minute or so introduction. I couldn't help reflect as I stepped into the spotlight in front of a capacity audience at this wonderful old theatre how different it was from my early speaking dates. The very first time I stepped outside the studio and in front of a live audience was a chastening experience. My collection of bad gags, stolen stories and unamusing anecdotes was met with near silence. It didn't help that no one was actually there to see me. Just as when you go to a live gig, no one really wants to watch the support act. Then I introduced former boxer Henry Cooper. He used the word 'fuck' in his first sentence and the entire audience fell about laughing. I felt like I had been hit by Henry's Hammer!

I loved the tour though. The old team was back together and the sold-out venues were proof of their popularity with young and old, men and women, regardless of their footballing allegiance. We performed to full houses from Southampton to Aberdeen. Time and again people would quietly whisper to me, '*Soccer Saturday* just isn't the same now'. I kept my counsel as I was still working for Sky and I didn't want word to get back that I had been critical of the company. After all, that company had given me the platform to lead the life I have lived.

All of the boys are brilliant raconteurs but in Southampton of course, Matt was the star of the show. People would

A bunch of old has-beens. The crowds that flocked to
'The Pundits' tour clearly thought Sky brought the curtain
down on them too soon.

turn up to see him at the opening of a letter. He is convinced
his use of social media cost him his job at Sky – I honestly
don't know if that was the case, but it may well have been.
Tiss was a Covid sceptic. He didn't believe in the vaccines
– and in fact was never inoculated himself. He questioned
the veracity of photos of bodies in the Ukraine. He high-
lighted threads that claimed 9/11 was a conspiracy. Those
views have certainly cost him a great deal of work in terms
of after-dinner speaking. He stood down from his role at St

Mary's as an ambassador for the club. As their greatest ever player, that must have been quite a sacrifice. I don't share his views in any way, shape or form. I understand that many people find his comments distasteful. But if he is willing to bear the consequences of his remarks, then I would defend his right to make them – no matter how bonkers they may seem. Needless to say on our tour, we would not be discussing anything like that but I always introduced him by saying, 'If you want to wind Tiss up, remind him he won ten fewer England caps than Carlton Palmer. And fifty-one less than Phil Neville – though he won more England B caps than them both put together. Or if you really, really want to wind him up, just tell him Covid and 9/11 really did happen.' And he accepted this with a smile.

In Aberdeen, Charlie Nicholas was the star. I had always thought of Charlie as ex-Celtic and Arsenal, forgetting his two and a half years at Pittodrie. Phil Thompson was adored anywhere close to his beloved Liverpool and they loved Paul Merson in Birmingham – or at least Aston Villa fans did. I was excited to see the queues winding around the streets of Birmingham when we appeared there. It was a much younger audience than usual too. It turned out they were there to see a British rapper called Aitch at the O2 Academy. We were a couple of hundred yards away at the Alexandra Theatre where there was a significantly smaller queue waiting to see Jay, Pee, Emm, Thommo and Charlie.

I also discovered a solution to overcrowding in British prisons. Put them all in the same Birmingham hotel that we stayed in, though many would complain about the size of the cells, or rooms, and the lack of anything in them apart from a bed. After the show, we headed out for dinner. Being Birmingham, it had to be curry. It was thoroughly mediocre, the highlight being when Charlie asked for a bottle of Sauvignon Blanc or something similar as we drank our Cobras and Kingfishers. The owner turned up with a bottle, whose recently applied label read 'Chateau Calcutta' or something similar. In fairness, it was clear straightaway that the contents had never been anywhere near France.

We had a lot of fun and not just on stage. When I arrived at a lovely seafront hotel in Southend, the owner said, because she loved watching me so much, she had given me the best room. It was gorgeous – big, with lovely furnishings and a large balcony with a wonderful sea view. When I met Phil and Charlie in the bar for a quick pre-performance drink, they looked a little crestfallen. Both their rooms they explained were tiny and overlooked the car park. I could not help but feel smug and needless to say I gloated over how much the owner loved me and had given me the best room in the place. I had gone so far down the garden path, I was in the nettle bed at the bottom before they told me they actually had rooms either side of mine, identical in size and with balconies overlooking the sea. 'You dick,' said Thommo succinctly. And I had to agree with him.

With five of us plus a comedian, Jed Stone, the cost of putting on 'The Pundits' tour was significant. Venues needed to be big and full to the rafters to make it pay. Nailing down dates that suited us all was tricky. Charlie had business commitments that made it difficult for him. By October 2023 it had run its course. Our final night was at the Wolverhampton Grand Theatre. It was a 1,200 sell-out. Disappointingly, the day before the event, the promoter rang me to tell me that Paul Merson had pulled out. He didn't elaborate on why and I did not ask, but I knew that there had to be a good reason.

In all the years I had known him, Merse, despite all his personal issues, had always been there when he said he would. I can honestly say he never, ever let me down. So I knew his absence was for a genuine reason. It was a body blow though as he had been manager of Walsall just seven miles away and even though that had been a testing eighteen months, he was still extremely popular in the area. Merse told me that when he was in charge at the Bescott, at the start of a season, he would write down the names of his best side and put it in his desk drawer. When things were at their toughest, he would take the list from the drawer and name that team in the next game. His name would be on any piece of paper that I put in my desk drawer whether it was to remind me of my best *Soccer Saturday* panel, best on-stage performers or just best people.

His place was taken by Steve Bull. The Wolves record goalscorer was a fine replacement – at least I think he was! Steve is the proud possessor of a strong Black Country accent. If people had problems understanding me when I first went to London, goodness knows what they would have made of Bully. He told a story about Gazza on inter-national duty – all I could do was think about how the hell the two of them managed to communicate with each other! Any road, he wor bostin in the view of the audience, who wos 'avin a rart loff. (*Translation: He was excellent and the crowd laughed loudly.*) Even without Paul, we got a standing ovation.

It was the end of 'The Pundits' tour. But in January I embarked on another theatre tour – this time on my own. Or almost. I needed someone to act as host, ask a few ques-tions and be funny (but not too funny). Michael McPherson suggested one or two names, Perry Groves for instance. I like Perry on the radio, but I don't really know him. I felt it needed to be someone that I already had a relationship with, even if at times that relationship could be a little spiky. I told Michael to call Bianca Westwood. She jumped at the chance to spend around thirty evenings with me. Ok, perhaps not jumped at the chance, but she was eventually persuaded. The fee may have helped. We decided on a dry run to see if the chemistry worked on stage. It was in Blythe in the North East. Dry run was not the correct term. Bianca was a little nervous. This was somewhere outside her comfort zone. She would be on stage first on her own introducing me in front of 300 people. We asked for a drink in the green room beforehand and someone arrived with four miniature bottles of wine which looked like they had been stolen from some local and not very salubrious hotel and tasted like it too. Michael went to buy more wine – a bottle of rosé for

With Bianca during the 'Me and Bee' tour. Or, as she preferred,
the Dad and Daughter tour.

madam, red for me. As Bee quaffed the rosé, she looked a
little more relaxed. I told her to give me a big build up, but
then take the piss a little. She didn't need asking twice.

'Ladies and Gentlemen,' she announced, glass of rosé still
in hand. 'Please welcome the man you have all come to see.
He has been called a legend and the best in the business.'
I couldn't help but smile secretly as I waited in the wings.
'He has also been called short, old and fat,' she continued.
It brought the house down. The first half of the show went
smoothly. Bianca had accidently left her glass on stage, so
spent the interval quaffing the rest from the bottle. She was
no longer nervous. She was just hammered. Still the show

went without a hiccup – apart from hers. We got a standing ovation. I knew she was right for the show.

And so we set off in January. Yet again the starting point was Southampton. We travelled the length and breadth of the nation from Truro and Yeovil and Christchurch in the south to Dundee in the north, from Scarborough and Lowestoft in the east to Liverpool and Runcorn in the west. The one-man show was now a one-man, one-woman show. Me and Bee. We sold out at venue after venue, while other big name sports stars were struggling to attract audiences of over a hundred. Promoter Michael McPherson decided demand was so great that we should do it again in the autumn. This time it'll be Bedford to Billingham, Kirkcaldy to Maidstone. I had only ever wanted to work on my local newspaper. Now I was travelling the nation with my own show. As Richard Littlejohn might have said, 'You couldn't make it up . . .'

The Games of My Life

REAL MADRID 4 v 1 ATLETICO MADRID

Champions League final, Estadio da Luz, Lisbon, 24 May 2014

Sky's coverage of the first ever one-city Champions League final was 20 minutes away from getting underway from a studio tucked near one corner of a stand at the Estadio da Luz, home of Benfica. And there was the problem. The studio was inside, but at that stage I was outside.

I had been inside, of course, rehearsing the one and three quarter hour build-up for much of the hot Lisbon afternoon and had been up and down the staircase, and in and out of the entrance more than once without problem. But minutes before we were due to go live, I was stranded outside. A stern Portuguese security guard, the same one I had passed several times already, initially giving him my best 'Bom Dia', had now decided my pass was not the correct one to use the entrance and staircase when I most needed to.

I'd left rehearsals because my two teenage sons had arrived at the stadium to see the biggest game of their lives and I had gone to find them as I had their tickets.

Normally I treat work as just that and don't bring my family to matches. But this was to be part of a family holiday as we would drive to the Algarve the following morning. I had foregone the usual pre-final, no expense spared slap-up dinner with the team and instead we ended up in a back street restaurant where the tiny frontage opened up into a huge banqueting-style hall awash with wooden bench tables. It was packed with local Portuguese people. There was no menu – the choice was pretty much steak, chicken or fish. And the wine list was very much red or white! It turned out to be a wonderful pre-match meal.

The tickets themselves had been like gold-dust and after booking flights and hotels for the boys and my wife and daughter, I had been let down a week before the game. The two tickets I had been promised – my wife Lizzie and daughter Olivia wanted to see Lisbon, not the game – were no longer available. Barney Francis, the managing director of Sky Sports, had saved the day by providing me with two spares for the boys. I didn't find out until afterwards that these were actually *his* tickets and my sons, Robbie and Matt would spend the day being dined like high-powered executives and sitting with UEFA dignitaries and television controllers during the game – if I had known I would have asked them to put in a good word for me! So after finding my lads and delivering them to the VIP lounge, I headed back to the studio. I had been cutting it fine but was relieved to know they were safe and inside the ground. I returned to the entrance I needed only to be stopped in my tracks by the immovable object of the security guard. I quickly realised neither 'Bom Dia' nor 'Don't you know who I am?' was going to work this time.

I had been all around the world to Olympic Games, World Athletics Championships, Commonwealth Games and previous Champions League finals and never come close to missing the start of a programme. I had almost missed the kick-off in a League Cup tie at Turf Moor when Burnley were playing Spurs on a foul night in Lancashire. Snow had turned into driving rain made even more unpleasant by a howling wind. As I went to enter the ground, I was stopped by a steward.

'Jeff lad, great to see you,' he said, as cheerfully as he could in the conditions. 'I just love Soccer Saturday. Never miss it when Burnley are away.' We chatted until I told him I needed to get into the studio. 'Nice to meet you then Jeff,' he said. 'You'll just need to show me your pass though before I can let you in!' I thought he was just having a laugh, but even though he knew exactly who I was and why I was there, he would not let me through. To be honest, it wasn't a great issue. I scuttled off to the fleet of TV trucks, picked up a pass and presented it to the same steward to gain access in good time.

But here in Lisbon was different. Time was against me. And so was the security guard. I remember Chris

Kamara being refused entry to a match in England because he didn't have a pass. 'This is my pass,' said Kammy, pointing at his own face. I had the suspicion that approach would not do the trick here. I rang the Sky production manager. Less than 15 minutes until we were on air and people were wondering where the hell I was! She came to the entrance but could not move the immovable object in dayglow orange that stood between me and Jamie Redknapp, Graeme Souness and Xabi Alonso, the suspended Real midfielder who was joining us at the start of the show. Then came a moment of genius. My production manager asked if her accreditation was the correct one to gain access to the studio. It was. And so in front of his very eyes, she took my pass, I took hers – complete with her name and her photo – and like magic, the guard waved me through! I got to my seat hot, sweaty and bothered. It was hardly the ideal preparation for Sky's biggest footballing night of the year.

The game itself was thankfully a lot better than my preparation. The atmosphere among the 61,000 almost exclusively Spanish crowd was as good-humoured as it had been all day in the Portuguese capital. We had travelled on the Lisbon underground with Real supporters singing at one end of a carriage and Atletico supporters doing the same at the other end. There was a carnival feel in the bars and the restaurants of the city with rivalry amongst the fans but no hostility.

The build-up to the game had been about Real's bid to win La Decima, their tenth European Cup. They had been waiting twelve years and suffered three semi-final defeats. But their crushing of Bayern Munich in the semis and their array of *Galacticos* – Ronaldo, Benzema, Modric, Bale (they liked him at Real then) and Ramos – made them favourites, even though their opponents had clinched the La Liga title just a week before.

Despite being champions, Atletico were still seen in most quarters as the poor relations when it came to football in Madrid. Real were rich and swaggering, Atletico humble. Fans at the Bernabeu were demanding and unforgiving while Atletico's were long-suffering and loyal. The contrast continued in the dug-out. Real were represented by the cool, sophisticated, seemingly unshakeable Carlo Ancelotti, Atletico by the snarling, street fighter who couldn't give a damn about what anyone thought about him, Diego Simeone.

The match itself was one of the most dramatic Champions League finals ever. Atletico led after 36 minutes through the uncompromising defender Diego Godin, who had scored against Barcelona a week earlier to seal Atletico's domestic title. From then on a red and white wall defied Real by fair means and foul, picking up seven yellow cards in the process. You would not have known from Ancelotti's expression if his team were winning or losing. Simeone, arms flying, exhorted his team to victory with screams and shouts. But in the

93rd minute and with his first Champions League trophy almost in his grip, he was silenced as Sergio Ramos rose above everyone to head home Luca Modric's corner to take the game to extra-time.

The rest was inevitable. Gareth Bale nodded Real ahead, Marcello slid a third under the diving Thibaut Courtois and Cristiano Ronaldo slotted home a penalty in the 120th minute to make it 4–1.

Atletico's team were tamed but not their manager. Simeone, believing a ball had been kicked at him, went on to the pitch looking to take revenge on the culprit and finished the night with a red card.

It had been an exhilarating game – one which I had almost missed. We stayed on the air for another hour with reaction to what we had seen in Lisbon that evening before I headed off into the cool night air to find my boys.

As I came to the bottom of the staircase, I dug deep into my Portuguese knowledge. '*Boa Noite*,' I said to the security guard, thankful that I didn't have the vocabulary to say what I really thought!

The Games of My Life

WINCHESTER CITY 0 v 1 WINCHESTER YOUTH
City of Southampton Youth League, Chilcomb Recreation
Ground, Hampshire, October 2017

This was a challenge that even Sir Alex Ferguson would have found daunting.

I had been involved in local football for a decade. Both my boys played schools football, with my younger son Matt joining a local club when he was seven years old. He was a goalkeeper who would briefly be recruited by Reading's academy. I was working so couldn't go to his first session at the Madejski but my wife did. I called her 15 minutes in to ask what they were doing. 'Running,' said Lizzie. Fifteen minutes later I called again. 'Still running,' was the response. The reply was the same the next couple of times I rang. Apparently they only got a ball out for the last 15 minutes. I spoke to Steve McClaren, then England manager, about this and suggested that the lack of a ball during a seven-year-old's football coaching sessions was perhaps one of the reasons why the national side was struggling! Within a few weeks, Matt had decided he would rather play *with* a ball and quit the academy.

Robbie, who is fifteen months older, started to play a couple of years later, a midfielder with a good engine and a good passing range. For years I went to both teams' training sessions, watched them every Sunday, ran the line and occasionally, when an official failed to turn up, would referee matches.

In that time I had seen the good, the bad and the ugly of youth football. A coach of another team, a likeable man whose sides played a lovely passing game, told me he was quitting. He had been head-butted by a parent – from his own team. His crime was to substitute the irate father's son to give others time on the pitch. They were under-11s!

At under-13s, an Eastleigh team had been coached to surround Matt at corners, with a player holding down each arm so he could not move. Yes, they coached them this! The team would kick the ball away whenever a free-kick was given against them and when my son kicked the ball out of play so an opposition player could be treated for an injury, the coach told his side not to give the ball back. At the end of the game, I marched over to their group of parents and suggested it would benefit their kids if they found a new team – or a new coach.

They didn't find the new coach and a couple of years later we played them again. Eastleigh were top of the table but Matt's team won 5–0. As our boys emerged triumphantly from the changing rooms a little later, some of the Eastleigh players were waiting. They had armed themselves with pieces of metal and bricks from a nearby skip. Our group of parents included a couple of bouncers and a senior policeman – as well as me of course – and the would-be assailants soon scattered when they saw us. I wrote to Eastleigh FC, their parent club in the National League, to complain but got a lip-service type of response.

At Millbrook one Sunday afternoon, a young referee needed the protection of the same group of dads after a group of men on the touchline had spent much of the afternoon drinking cans of Tennent's lager. All this is happening in leafy Hampshire, hardly one of the trouble spots of the United Kingdom. No wonder we struggle to get refs.

Mind you, my boys' teams didn't always help themselves. I remember Robbie having a word during the course of a game one cold December morning with an aggressive, threatening, mouthy young skinhead in the opposition midfield. Robbie had told him, 'You must be really hard, wearing gloves.' He then spent the rest of the game keeping as far away from him as possible.

The boys' teams were both in the Southampton Tyro League and played in different age groups. But at seventeen, they graduated into the City of Southampton League. It meant that in their second season Winchester Youth, Robbie's team, would play Winchester City,

Matt's team. It was the first time they had ever played a competitive game against each other.

To complicate matters, I now coached Robbie's team with another dad, Rob Lane. We had a decent enough side, though there were challenges as they were eighteen or almost eighteen years old. Would our centre-half, who had been seen at a bus stop in Winchester at midnight the previous night with a crate of Heineken, turn up? And if he did what condition would he be in? How could I drop our tall, handsome but not very talented midfielder when he showed up for a match with his new girlfriend? Do I start our best player after he admitted that he had been to an all-night party and had not been to bed?

Matt's team on the other hand were a year younger, less likely to be out boozing and more significantly most were much better players. They were top of the league with a 100 per cent record.

On the way to the game, Robbie said his main hope was not to concede double figures. To be honest, knowing we had scraped together a bare eleven, I felt the same.

But at least I knew how they played. In a pre-match talk that Pep Guardiola has never given (though Jose Mourinho may have) I told them how we would play. Let their back four have it and do not press them. Make the defenders try and pass through us. Double up on their most talented midfield players. Our full-backs were not to risk getting out of position by crossing the halfway line under any circumstances. If we had a chance, slide the ball in behind their giant centre-halves on the floor for Alex Ladkin, our predatory striker. These tactics I felt should guarantee nothing worse than a 6–0 hammering.

Then shortly before kick-off, the news came through that the referee would not be turning up. I could feel all eyes on me. City coach Simon Welsh, who I had known for years, approached me and asked me if I would ref the game.

'But Simon,' I pleaded, 'I coach one of the teams and have a boy on each side. It is impossible.' I was determined not to do it.

Simon played his final card. 'But if you don't Jeff, the game will be off.' I gathered all the players around and they all agreed they wanted me to referee the game. Against my better judgement, I did. As normal, a dad from either side ran (possibly an exaggeration) the line.

Amazingly by half-time, the game was goalless. We had not been out of our own half admittedly, but they had created next to nothing.

City flung forward after forward on. We stuck with what we had. We had no choice. All our boys had started. There were some close shaves. A goalmouth scramble, but it was impossible to tell whether the ball was over the line. Then a goal against us – but the linesman had his flag up for offside. After 70 minutes,

Robbie ran past me and said, 'Dad, we might get something out of this!'

Then, five minutes from time, the impossible happened. One of our players slid a ball behind their central defenders for Alex Ladkin to run on to. We had not had a shot on goal during the entire game. I was torn. I wanted Alex to score, but I wanted Matt to save it. Alex drilled the ball into the bottom corner of the net.

Now things were getting feisty. Some would say the referee had lost control. Alex was through again, only to be hauled down by the centre-half. Last man, a clear goal-scoring opportunity, it had to be a red card. But I knew the kid who had committed the offence and just could not do it. Ninety minutes were up. I knew that for the Stelling household a draw was the best result by far. Into added time . . . three minutes, four, five, six. I gave City as long as I dared, but they could not equalise.

As my team celebrated, the City players shook my hand. Some were fine with me, others did it grudgingly. Matt did not speak to me for a full week. When he finally did, he told me I had cheated because I knew the strengths and weaknesses of the City players and I had shamelessly passed this on to players in my team. I think seven years on, I may have been forgiven.

A few months later, with City having dropped no more points, we tried the same thing again. At 0–0, midway through the second half, our right-back chased out of defence and into their half for the first time in either match. He lost the ball, they played it into the space he had left and scored. I was secretly pleased. I knew that honours shared over the two games would heal any rifts in the Stelling household.

17

BEING JEFF STELLING

'You look like the bloke off the telly, you know the bloke who shouts out the football results at a million miles an hour,' said my newly acquired, newly inebriated companion.

I was walking back late at night from a meal at a friend's restaurant in Albufeira in Portugal. A man, half-consumed Sagres in hand, tottered towards me to ask me if I knew the whereabouts of 'The Strip'. I did. He was heading in exactly the wrong direction. My route back to the calm of Olhos de Agua, the one-time fishing village where I was staying, took me directly past the bottom of the notorious two-kilo-metre-long stretch of bars and clubs, frequented by hordes of tourists dressed as brides, schoolgirls or supermen. Men and women on stag and hen nights would wear matching t-shirts, all adorned somewhere on their clothing with their names. For anyone over thirty, 'The Strip' is to be avoided at all costs. Of course I only know this because friends have been there! When I reached it, I would always keep my head down and increase my pace for fear of being recognised. I knew it was about 15 minutes' walk away so I told Colin to

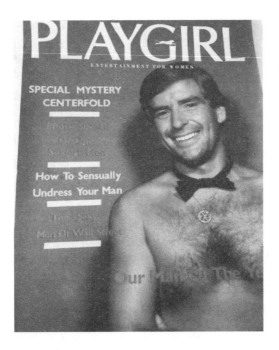

This was taken several weeks ago . . .

follow me ('Colin' was emblazoned in red across the back of his yellow t-shirt). He had somehow been separated from his fellow stag-ees.

Colin wanted to chat. I wanted my bed. It was late and I didn't want to talk to him about being on TV, *Soccer Saturday*, Chris Kamara, Pep Guardiola or anything to do with football. But his face was now a nose length away from mine as he became more and more convinced of my minor celebrity status. 'You are Jeff, aren't you?' he slurred. 'Or you look just like him.' There was only one thing to do. Lie. 'I am his brother Henry actually,' I said. 'A lot of people say we look alike. But I can't stand him – or football!' As the yards ticked by towards his debauched destination, I painted a picture of myself as an accountant living a quiet and lonely life (which fitted the bill as I was alone on holiday) and having nothing to do with my smug, flash, TV star brother. 'We don't even exchange cards at Christmas,' I told him. 'A waste of the price of a stamp.' The further we walked, the more convinced he was of my identity. As we parted, he shook my hand. He waved me off with, 'Thanks Henry. My god though, you do look like your bastard brother!' and headed off to tell his mates he had met Henry Stelling. It was naughty of me. Over the decades, people I have met have been unfailingly polite. I have to pinch myself to remember I am a council house boy from Hartlepool when people ask me for a selfie. It is just a slightly strange life when everybody feels they know you, even though they really don't.

On another occasion in Portugal, my son was celebrating his sixteenth birthday with a group of friends in Manzo, one of our favourite restaurants. At about 11 o'clock, I arrived to pay the bill. As I walked towards them, a diner recognised me. Shocked that Jeff Stelling was in the same place as him, his head and body twisted as his eyes followed me. Until his chair toppled backwards and he ended up on the floor of the busy restaurant. Cue hysteria among those he was with – and my son and his mates. He was one person who didn't bother asking for a photo.

I have been mistaken for many people. Usually Geoff Shreeves or Richard Keys. I don't mind the former, not so keen on being called the latter! I was once misidentified as

Trevor Brooking. Yes, that 6 feet tall, slender, ex-England international footballer Trevor Brooking. The only thing we have in common is that neither of us can head a ball! Recently, I met a chap who thought he recognised me, but just couldn't quite nail it down. His opening gambit was 'You are the feller from Sky . . . Sky . . . Sky.' 'Sports,' I added helpfully. 'Yes, the feller on Gillette . . . Gillette . . . Gillette.' '*Soccer Saturday*,' I finished. 'Yes, and you support, don't tell me, don't tell me . . . Wakefield!' he announced triumphantly. I realised this was the first time I had ever been mistaken for Wakefield native, Chris Kamara. An easy mistake to make. Or perhaps not. Most of the time, the recognition is good fun. I have even had photos taken with Darlington support-ers. People are often keen to tell me they have watched me all of their life, which is of course a compliment, but when it comes from a thirty-year-old, it does make me realise that I have gone from spring chicken to old goat in what seems no time at all. The truth is that the time to worry is when you have become such an old goat that nobody wants your photo. Thankfully, that hasn't happened to me yet.

Everywhere I go there are still cheery shouts of 'Un-believable Jeff!' People light-heartedly talk about my height (you look taller on telly), my weight (you look fatter on telly, phew) and my voice (we can recognise it from a mile off). They'll ask about my teeth (are they your own?) and my complexion (have you had Botox?). Many years ago Danny Baker even wrote a newspaper column suggesting I had six toes on each foot! It is important to take every good-natured comment in the spirit it was meant.

But sometimes people can push it too far. I had just been served dinner in a favourite restaurant one night when a man came off the street and asked for a selfie. Dinner is sacrosanct territory for me so politely I told him I was just starting my meal. The table next to me was empty, so he pulled up a chair and said, 'No problem. I can wait till you have finished,' as he stared across at me.

In 2013, I went to the Rose Bowl with my two sons one day to watch a Twenty20 match between England and Australia. At the change of innings, so many people were queuing for an autograph and blocking other spectators' views that eventually we had to leave. Thankfully, we had seen Aaron Finch score an incredible 156 in 63 balls.

Football fans are invariably really good natured with me, especially when my team is losing to theirs 'Stelling, Stelling, what's the score?' is a FAQ. Quite a few years ago I went to see Sunderland play in a pre-season friendly in Albufeira (I know, I know, this could be judged as going a step too far, certainly in the eyes of Mrs Stelling). Once I had been noticed, the fans cheerfully chanted 'Stelling, Stelling give us a wave!' But when I needed a mid-game visit to the highly visible toilets, they let me know they had spotted me with 'We know where you are going, we know where you are going!' And when we left ten minutes before the end to maintain an element of family harmony by having dinner before all the restaurants closed, all I could hear was 'We can see you sneaking out!'

I've never courted headlines over my years on TV – unless it has been to promote a good cause like Prostate Cancer UK or a lost cause, like Hartlepool United (just joking Mr Chairman!) Sometimes I have made them accidentally, such as when I fell in my lounge and hit my eye on a brass door handle. Even those watching in black and white could see I was black and blue. Or sometimes you have to put certain people right as I did when Piers Morgan was having a dig at Mikel Arteta. 'Row', 'Feud' and 'Vendetta' all appeared in the headlines when in truth it was just a bit of fun. But sometimes you need to beware of your nearest and dearest. Pigs-in-blankets-gate was a reminder to me.

It was just before Christmas 2022 when I made the schoolboy error of leaving my mobile within reach of my sons Robbie and Matt as I popped out to the kitchen to grab a beer. When I picked up my phone half an hour later, I was trending on Twitter. A tweet posted in my name read, 'I love cooking Christmas dinner in the buff.' Pictured was a tray of thirty or so pigs-in-blankets. Except there was an imposter. There, camouflaged and nearly hidden in the corner, was a penis. I cried with laughter to be honest but then deleted it quickly. The damage though was done. On Boxing Day virtually every national newspaper ran the story on the front page. Kammy warned people to inspect their pigs-in-blankets carefully before eating them. I explained to viewers what had happened. Hartlepool fan Robbie would be punished by having to wear a Darlington shirt. Brighton fan Matt would have his season ticket replaced by one for Crystal Palace. Just for a little while I wished I was Henry Stelling again.

18

THE TEAM OF MY LIFE

Darius Rucker summed it up perfectly. 'There are two times of year for me – the football season and waiting for the football season.' As he was lead singer for the American band Hootie and the Blowfish, I suspect he was talking about a different type of football. But it is very relevant to the game we love as well.

Football has dominated my life. Playing in local leagues until I was forty (well, turning up anyway), supporting my team Hartlepool United, watching my two sons play and of course being involved with the game through my job. I watch football from the Champions League down to the National League, the World Cup down to the EFL Trophy. I read the football pages in national and local newspapers, football websites and football statistics sites. I read football magazines and listen to football podcasts. There's a really good one that's come out in the last year or so called *Football's Greatest!* There has barely been a day when I haven't thought about football. So I decided that I would pick a team of my life – players who have influenced me in one way or another or perhaps just someone I loved watching. In fact it is a squad, as we know the game is a squad game these days!

The first of my two goalkeepers is ex-England, Liverpool and Spurs keeper RAY CLEMENCE. Of course he was a fine goalkeeper, but it's the man I remember more. I didn't know him well but at the end of my twenty-ninth walking marathon for Prostate Cancer UK, Ray was there to greet me at the Tottenham Hotspur Stadium along with my friend Lloyd Pinder. Both were suffering from the illness. Lloyd had taken part in many walks but was not well enough this time. Neither Ray nor Lloyd would show their suffering. Both would say they were fine. They would die within two months of each other. Less than a year after Ray's death, I had the pleasure of walking a marathon with his son Stephen and his daughter-in-law Suzanne Collins, along with four of Ray's grandchildren. Ray's wife Vee met us at Anfield. We took a short walk to Wylva Road where he is immortalised in a mural. Alongside are the words of Bill Shankly: 'Ray has everything. He's quick, he doesn't want to be beaten, he's just a great goalkeeper.' If he is good enough for Shanks, he is good enough for me.

My second goalkeeper is MATT STELLING! When his older brother Robbie and I went for a kickabout, Matt would frequently go in goal and he was pretty good. When he first went to school, I told him to tell his sports teacher that he was a midfielder or a defender, anything but a goalie. When the first school team was named, he was in it – as keeper! It was the start of years of anguish. It is hard enough being a keeper, but even harder being a keeper's dad. But he was tough and he was brave. In a local cup game, he was kicked hard in the head as he plunged at the feet of a rival forward. He wanted to continue, but clearly something was wrong when we saw him standing 10 yards to the right of his goal believing he was between the posts. There were no concussion rules in those days. We spent the evening in A&E. Matt broke his nose in another collision. His team had a big cup game coming up so we investigated the possibility of getting him a protective mask to play in. He was thirteen at the time! We couldn't get the mask, but he played anyway. I had to look away every time an opposing player challenged him. In the last game of another season, he broke the thumb of his right hand. I rang his mum with the bad news. When I pointed out that it was the last game of the season so he would not miss any football, she erupted. I had forgotten he was due to take his GCSEs in a few days. Without the use of his right thumb, he would not be able to hold a pen. Thanks goodness for laptops!

My first defender is the Welshman GARETH JELLEY-MAN who obligingly got the first red card of his career at Oxford late one Saturday afternoon, which gave me the chance to use my long prepared line: 'Gareth Jelleyman has been sent off for Mansfield, let's hope he hasn't thrown a wobbly.' Scores were flooding in at the time, but I didn't care if Manchester United had conceded in the last minute. That could wait until I delivered the line. It also gave me the title of one of my earlier books.

I'm not sure if PHIL THOMPSON or GORDON MCQUEEN were on the panel that day. I went to Gordon's funeral in 2023, gone far too young at just seventy. Big Go-go, as we all knew him, was a fine footballer but he was also one of the funniest men you will ever meet. During a medical before an ankle operation, he was asked how many units of alcohol he usually consumed. He admitted to thirty. 'That's not bad Mr McQueen, just above the recommended twenty-eight a week,' said the doctor who I imagine was taken aback when Go-go informed him he meant thirty units a day! By chance he and his wife Yvonne spent a week with us in the same hotel in Barbados. My kids were too young to eat out, but the McQueens would turn up every evening with a couple of bottles of Champagne to share on the terrace. Most days we would see grey/green, shaking, unwell young people wandering the resort. It would turn out they had spent the previous night drinking with Go-go. Our stats man David Todd was a similar colour when he took on Gordon in the Raw-Egg-Eating Challenge Cup. Gordon could swallow copious numbers with no effect – this was a bad miscalculation from a stats man! I hadn't realised that Gordon's life had run parallel to his best mate Joe Jordan. They were in digs together in Leeds, played in the first team together, both moved to Manchester United and married within a week of each other. Go-go was Joe's best man, Joe was Gordon's.

Phil Thompson's influence has been as a sort of father figure. He will hate that but he is fourteen months older than me after all. During the show we have often argued, mainly because Thommo bleeds red, and will never, ever criticise his beloved Liverpool. But that loyalty is not confined to his football club. He is a loyal friend too. If I was in trouble, he would be pretty much the first person I would call. I have never heard him have a bad word about anyone – well, two people in fact. But those two names will remain between me and him. I was pleased for him when he left the show to become No. 2 to Gerard Houllier but gutted for myself and the show. Thankfully he returned and though he left before me, we remain good mates.

Three defenders is enough. My first midfielder is RAY WILKINS, the former England, Chelsea and Manchester United star. I loved the fact that on the field he understood the value of not giving the ball away. Ray did all his giving off the field. I worked with him on Sky's Champions League coverage and while he would criticise players during his co-commentary, he did it in the gentlest way possible. 'Stay on your feet, young fella,' would be as harsh as he would get. He supported the Prostate Cancer UK marathons, often walking with those at the back of the group to encourage and cajole. Midway through one walk, I found him sitting in the ambulance room, his feet swollen and blistered. He hadn't told anyone around him that he was suffering. When he was younger, my elder son Robbie was misguided enough to think he was a Chelsea fan before he learned the joys of Hartlepool United. I rang Ray to ask him if we could get a couple of tickets to a game. Ray asked us to turn up early.

When we did, Ray was there to meet us. He had arranged lunch for us, a guided tour of the stadium and best of all, as Roman Abramovic wasn't going to be at the match, he had arranged for us to sit in his seats. I was an oligarch for a day.

I tried to impress on ROBBIE STELLING the importance of not giving the ball away. Not all his coaches agreed. In a Southampton Tyro League game where his side were taking a bit of pasting, he rolled the ball back to his keeper from 30 yards. His coach promptly subbed him. My explanation that it was important to keep the ball came in for criticism in harsher terms than Ray Wilkins would ever have dealt out. Robbie was a central midfielder, but he had played goalkeeper, centre-half, full-back and right-wing, so was a team player. He was also captain of the team that I coached (well, what do you expect?). In the penultimate game of one season our side, which was very hit and miss, depending on how many were nursing hangovers, was playing a team who needed to win to have a chance of the league. With minutes left we were leading 2–1. I called Robbie over to the touchline and told him to get as far over to the other side of the pitch as possible. I would sub him and he would walk the entire width of the field to kill some time. What followed was a Gielgud-like performance. As the ball went out, I called 'Ref, sub please. Robbie off you come.' His head fell as if in disbelief as he stood absolutely still. Then he took off the captain's armband and slowly trudged 20 yards to give it to a team-mate. Next he jogged to the opposition captain to offer a none-too-welcome handshake. Then he headed to the centre circle to shake the hand of the referee, before finally walking towards the touchline at a snail's pace. I was a proud dad! Thirty seconds later, the full-time whistle sounded and we had won. I know you may want to tell me this is not the right attitude, but you would be talking to someone who may, or may not, have told his daughter to squeeze the opposition captain's hand as hard as she possibly could before the start of a school netball match.

When I left Sky, one of the gifts I was given was a Subbuteo size JAMES MADDISON figure. It had become a running joke that I loved him (as a player obviously). I just could not understand why he was not in the England squad when he seemed to have the lot. His movement was great, he took up good positions, he could run with the ball, he was perceptive and he took brilliant free-kicks. Oh god, it is sounding like I loved him, isn't it? He talks well in interviews and though he doesn't blow his own trumpet, I know he frequently gives to good causes. I have never met him, but I would be shocked if he wasn't one of the good guys. Anyway, he gets in as my current favourite Premier League player.

My next midfielder was the man dubbed the next Marco Van Basten when he was a teenager at Sheffield Wednesday. RITCHIE HUMPHREYS never quite hit those heights but still had a long and solid career. He was voted Player of the Century – quite an accolade – at Hartlepool United and among a club record 544 appearances were two that stand out in my mind for different reasons. In a League Two play-off semi-final penalty shootout, Ritchie's spot-kick turned out to be decisive. He hit the underside of the crossbar, the ball bounced down on to the line, hit the post and span away from goal. Cheltenham went through instead. This was two days before Hartlepool elected H'angus the Monkey as the new mayor by the way! Three seasons later in a League One play-off semi-final at Prenton Park, Humphreys stepped up again in a shootout. He hadn't taken a penalty since his miss at Cheltenham. He showed Stuart Pearce-like strength of character to bury the kick and help his side through. In his years at Victoria Park, he played in every position except goalkeeper and later he would fill another different role when he became chairman of the PFA.

I watched the epic Spurs against Ajax Champions League semi-final second leg on an iPad with DECLAN RICE. I was hosting West Ham's annual awards at a London hotel and while dinner was going on, we went to the green room to watch the game. He was so unassuming it was hard to believe he was on his way to being English football's next big thing. I told him when he was past his prime I could fix him up with a game at Hartlepool. I think that will be a long time coming!

GEORGE BEST was just as unassuming. I had first met him at a charity game in South East London. He nutmegged me and when I turned round to chase, he nutmegged me in the opposite direction. George's many attributes didn't stretch to reliability and during his years on *Soccer Saturday* we always had a substitute guest ready to appear if George didn't turn up. If he hadn't been a footballer, he could have been an escapologist. His wife, Alex, would put him in a cab and tell the driver to go straight to the studios and not stop. George would persuade him to pause at the Phene pub in Chelsea and promptly disappear. If he did reach Sky, there was no guarantee he would make it to his seat. At least once, I left him in make-up at 11.45 – and didn't see him again until 6 o clock at the local rugby club. George was soft spoken, almost shy, on the panel. But it didn't matter. He was George Best, one of the greatest players ever to grace the game. My boss Vic Wakeling promised him a job for life. George had survived so many health scares, we all thought he would live forever. The day he died in 2005, aged just fifty-nine, was one of the saddest ever for me and all lovers of football.

When my JAMES BROWN doll made his first appearance on *Soccer Saturday* dancing and singing 'I Feel Good', everyone was taken by surprise. I had celebrated James' goals for Hartlepool with a jig that would have embarrassed the King of Soul. But we didn't do embarrassment on *Soccer Saturday*. We took the celebration to a whole new level when a well-wisher gave me the doll to use on the show. I had told no one about it and smuggled it away under my desk to be produced to serenade James if he scored. Midway through the second half Phil Thompson was updating us on, I believe, Manchester United's game when Brown scored. Out came the dancing doll to the astonishment of everyone. To be honest, I almost forgot to press the button that makes him sing! Every time James scored from then on, the boys would yell 'Get the doll out, get the doll out!' For eight years, the doll became a fifth panellist! Poor James was a lovely footballer, but he didn't always feel good. Injuries blighted his career and eventually forced his premature retirement.

Another who got regular mentions during the show was KENNY DEUCHAR, the Good Doctor. He managed to combine being a qualified doctor with banging in goals for a number of Scottish clubs, notably Gretna. Every time he scored we would reference 'the Good Doctor'. As he scored sixty-three in ninety-three at Gretna and once broke the second division goalscoring record, the Good Doctor appeared more often than anyone for a few seasons. We featured his Granny Mae who watched the show religiously to follow her grandson's fortunes. Some weeks it was more like 'At home with the Deuchars' than a football programme. Kenny moved on loan at Northampton and I went to see him play at Brentford in 2007. When he played his final game for the club, Northampton fans dubbed it 'Doctor's Day' and wore white jackets in his honour. I met Kenny again at a hospital in Scotland. I still have the stethoscope he gave me that day. Just as well as at my age it is always worth checking the heart is still beating. Still, if I ever need an appointment with a GP, I know I would be guaranteed one with Kenny. And after all, he is a good doctor!

Dickie Davis produced a feature a couple of years ago with one of my favourite players from my second favourite boyhood club (I was allowed two clubs when I was eight or nine years old!) The club was Burnley and the player was

DAVE THOMAS. I had never been to Burnley and had no real idea where it was in the country. But when I wrote to top division clubs asking for old programmes, photos and autographs, Burnley always sent a bumper bundle. In the 60s and 70s they had some fine players too. Steve Kindon would burst down the wing like an Olympic 100-metre runner, Frank Casper would ghost into wonderful positions, Martin Dobson was the original Rolls-Royce midfielder, there was the Welsh wizard Leighton James and out-and-out winger Dave Thomas. He would invariably be shinpad-less with socks down at his ankles as he twisted and turned his way through defences. I was beguiled by him. Like George Best, the more opponents kicked him, the better he would perform. He would go on to play for Queens Park Rangers, Everton and England. Dickie was visiting him because he was losing his sight. He suffered from glaucoma and had literally no peripheral vision. He could not manage without his guide dog and could no longer watch football. But rather than feel sorry for himself, Dave was more concerned about others and was helping raise money to help provide guide dogs, which can cost well over £50,000 to support through their working lifespan. His humility was touching, his determination inspirational. They say never meet your heroes. I have never met Dave, but I would take that chance given the opportunity.

KEVIN ELLISON was the sort of player you hated when he was playing against you, but I always said I would have loved him to play for my team. He admits that it was part of his game that on the pitch he was a horrible so-and-so. And he was a big, bald-headed bruiser (no offence, Kev) who would use his elbows and his tongue to wind up opponents. He had fourteen clubs but it was when he joined Morecambe that I really began to notice him. He didn't actually score that often against Hartlepool, but he was always trouble with a capital T. As the years rolled on I became fascinated by his longevity. He had looked forty, long before he was forty (no offence again, Kev) and when he parted company with Morecambe at that age I assumed he would retire. But he played as a triallist at Newport and despite getting injured, earned a contract aged forty-one. That season he became the oldest goalscorer in a play-off game when at forty-two years old he struck from 25 yards for County against Forest Green Rovers.

While I would have liked to have had Ellison in my team, I wouldn't have paid to have him in my team. But with LUKE JAMES that is exactly what I did – or rather tried to. When Luke notched his first goal at seventeen years old for Hartlepool, he became the youngest player to score for the club. He was a livewire, with boundless energy who chased lost causes and eventually moved to Peterborough United in a £500,000 deal. Things didn't quite work out and in 2016, he found his way back to Victoria Park as a loanee and rejoined permanently in 2018. He had lost none of his pace or will to win and became pivotal to Pools' hopes of getting promotion from the National League back to the Football League under Dave Challinor. So I was shocked when I heard he hadn't agreed a new deal. I rang the manager and asked how much he believed it would take for Luke to stay. He was a North East boy with a wife and young child. Dave reckoned an extra £10,000 a year would be enough. 'Tell the chairman I will pay the extra 10k and tell Luke he can have it monthly or in a lump sum,' I said. I had never volunteered to pay part of a player's wages before and haven't since. Soon after, Luke joined Barrow. The chairman had rejected my offer on the basis that others would want pay parity. But every team has a star player who earns more than the rest.

PAUL MERSON would have been the top earner at a couple of his clubs, I imagine. The Magic Man was just that on the pitch – magic. He is like that off the pitch too – magic. I sat next to him for years on *Soccer Saturday*, have worked with him at theatre shows and dinners and we have never had a cross word – not even about gambling, which I have touched on elsewhere in this book. As a pundit, he can't pronounce names and gets his phrases jumbled but he is brilliantly funny and unafraid to say what he thinks, even if the rest of the panel and all the viewers disagree with him. It is a great quality, which not many pundits possess. Paul has had bigger battles in his life than worrying about people disagreeing with his opinion. Until fairly recently, Merse played Sunday morning football at Wormwood Scrubs in London. One day he told me he was going to be sub. 'Sub mate, you? I wouldn't bother going!' was my reaction, prima donna that I am. 'We all have to take our turn Jeff,' was his response. I think that tells you lots about Paul Merson. Just a really good bloke.

Paul Merson sits in the seat next to the presenter on *Soccer Saturday*, previously occupied by George Best, Matt Le Tissier and my final squad member – though he would never have accepted being a squad player! Without RODNEY MARSH, I don't think the show would still be on the air now. It was – and is – a football show with no football, where a group of pundits tell you what you are missing. It doesn't sound that appealing. It needed a spark. It needed someone to make waves. It needed someone to cause headlines. In Rodney they had exactly the right man. He could be outrageous, outlandish and opinionated, which was exactly what the show needed, and he was never dull. Some weeks we would go through a sort of verbal Paso Doble. And we both knew the steps. Me: 'What do you think Rodney?' Him: 'Why are you asking me?' Me: 'Because I want to ask you Rodney.' Him: 'Why don't you ask one of the others?' Me: 'Because you are being paid to be on the panel and offer your views.' Him: 'What was the question again?' Rodney was great fun to work with. He wanted to be the star of the show, just as he had been so often as a player – and he was! *Soccer Saturday* started to get media coverage and acquired what the press would call a cult following. Then, in 2005 Rodney was sacked by Sky. It was nothing to do with our show but over an insensitive remark concerning the Asian Tsunami. Sky had hired him to make headlines but sadly he had created one too many.

The Games of My Life

BOCA JUNIORS 1 v 2 ATLETICO TUCUMAN

La Bombonera, Buenos Aires, Argentina, 21 February 2019

I had flown to Buenos Aires to deliver my son Matt and his friend Jake some new underpants.

A little extreme you may think, but it was how I ended up watching a game at one of the most atmospheric, famous and dangerous football grounds in the world.

La Bombonera is in the district of Boca, which all tourist guides will tell you only to visit as part of an organised group and during the day; never under any circumstances risk going there at night. This was a night match.

Matt and Jake had been on a gap year tour of South America. After a month in Brazil, they were heading for Argentina when the SOS came through. Send Out Smalls. I had a better idea. I told them I would bring them personally. I had never been to South America and this was a perfect opportunity. So after *Soccer Saturday* had finished that same week, I drove to Gatwick and jumped on a Norwegian Air flight to the Argentinian capital.

I had booked us all into a five-star hotel to provide them with a little luxury for a few days. I arrived first,

In the gods at La Bombonera, scarier
than a Hartlepool fan in Darlington.

in time to warn the concierge that the other two guests
would not be their usual clientele. To be honest, their smell
preceded them!

I loved everything about Buenos Aires. We visited the
Recoleta Cemetery where Eva Peron is buried: this city of
intricately decorated mausoleums truly is one of the wonders of the world. We politely explained to an elderly man
that we could not sign his petition for the Malvinas to be
returned to Argentina. Never mind dancing in the streets
of Total Network Solutions, they literally do dance in the
streets in the Argentinian capital city – there are open-air
Tango classes everywhere. We ate steaks the size of Razor

Ruddock, downed the local beer from two-litre bottles and drank Malbec until our complexions were as red as the wine. Then my son told me that he had booked tickets for the Boca game the following night.

This was my first visit to South America and I had read all the warnings about safety. The truth is that most of the time I felt safer there than in London. I will admit though to being more than a little apprehensive yet secretly pleased that we might see a game at one of the world's most famous, or possibly notorious venues. The tickets had been booked with an organised group, which made me feel a little more secure, and using my credit card, which made me feel a whole lot poorer.

We were given an address in the San Telmo area of the city where the group would meet before the game. We decided to check it out the day before. As we walked from the nearest underground station towards the meeting point, it was noticeable that the armed police that you see on virtually every street corner in BA were absent. The area was a little off the tourist track and very quiet.

We turned a corner and 100 yards ahead were six or seven teenagers sitting on doorway steps, each with a purple slash in their hair. It didn't take a genius to work out they were gang members. They stared, but nothing more, as we walked past and discovered a huge, signless wooden door, barred and closed now, but our destination the following day. It wasn't altogether encouraging. We decided the following evening we would take a taxi to get to the pick-up point.

As we clambered out of the cab on match night and in through the giant door, it was like stepping into another world – a cavernous, atmospheric room with pulsating music, packed with drinkers and diners. We were led to the back of the main dining area where we met our thirty-strong group of football fans from every corner of the world.

When it was time to leave, we were led to two minibuses. Away supporters were barred at games in Argentina because of the levels of violence and numbers of deaths at matches, so to get into La Bombonera we were given identity cards belonging to home fans. I was slightly concerned to see mine was in the name of Maria someone-or-other, but was told not to worry.

In the La Boca twilight, our guides led us towards the ground with a quick diversion into a house on the main drag into the stadium. No alcohol is allowed near the ground, but in the kitchen were cases of beer, available at an inflated price. This was a well-oiled operation in every sense.

As we continued towards the ground I remember telling one of the guides that this wasn't as threatening as I had expected and nothing like going to Millwall against West Ham at the original Den. 'It is ok now,' he said, 'but after the match this is no-man's land.' A garrison of armed police surrounded the ground. We were searched and moved towards the point where our ID cards would be checked. One of the guides approached first and, without a glance at our cards, we were all told to hurry through.

We clambered up stairs to our positions, high in one of the three precipice-like stands that tower above the pitch, gazing across to the much smaller flat-roofed stand opposite that helps give the ground its nickname of 'The Chocolate Box'. Huge wire fences separated the 48,000 fans from the playing area and, more importantly, separated us from the Ultras in the next section of the ground.

Of course, this was where it all really started for one of the world's greatest – and ultimately most tragic – players Diego Maradona. It is ok to mention 'The Hand of God' from the 1986 World Cup because the locals viewed it as just that. Maradona was their god. But using the word cheat would be more than a little inadvisable.

The star attraction for Boca that night was Carlos Tevez, the former West Ham, Man United, Man City and Juventus star, who had started his career there almost two decades earlier. Mauro Zarate, who had a spell at Birmingham City was also in their side, but in truth this was a far from vintage Boca team. Even their fanatical fans' expectations had been lowered. The opposition had travelled 800 miles from the north-west province of Tucuman and were just below Boca in the table.

The standard to be honest was not great, Championship level at best. Even with his best days behind him, Tevez was the standout player. But the fans sang from the first minute to the last. And I mean sang. They belted it out. There must be a heck of a market in throat lozenges around the ground. It was deafening. When Tucuman took the lead early, the frenetic atmosphere became a fraction more subdued, but it was cranked up again when the home team equalised. But when Tucuman striker David Barbona scored to put the visitors ahead again, it was almost too much for some fans, who were now clambering up the wire fences. I am not sure what they would have done if they had reached the top as there was a drop of 30 feet or more on the other side, but I guess a show of bravado never did anyone's reputation any harm.

The full-time whistle went and our group headed as quickly as we could through no-man's land to the minibuses and sanctuary back at the San Telmo bar, having experienced one of the great grounds, if not great games, in world football.

The Games of My Life

HARTLEPOOL UNITED 1 v 1 TORQUAY UNITED
AET (Hartlepool win 5–4 on penalties)
National League play-off final,
Ashton Gate, Bristol, 19 June 2021

It is not easy to see your team relegated from the Football League. It is even harder when you are on live TV. That's what happened to Hartlepool United in 2017. The brief but calamitous reign of former Wolves and Southampton manager Dave Jones had seen the team slip from seven points clear of relegation to two points short of safety when the club sacked him and put Matthew Bates in charge for the last two games. Defeat in the first of those two meant that on the last day of the season, Pools needed to beat title-chasing Doncaster Rovers and hope Newport County failed to beat Notts County.

The games kicked off at 5.30 after the rest of the day's fixtures, so *Soccer Saturday* stayed on air to cover them. At half-time, with Pools 1–0 behind and Newport leading 1–0, I abandoned any attempt at neutrality and, despite the fact that polyester is unflattering to the fuller frame, ripped off my jacket and presented the second half in my blue and white Pools shirt. It seemed to work

Bates appeared to have lost his mind when he brought on a sub, eighteen-year-old Devante Rodney who hadn't pulled up any saplings let alone trees in his time at Victoria Park. Notts County had equalised at Rodney Parade. Pools needed two goals in 17 minutes to preserve their 96-year unbroken run in the EFL. And somehow in the 74th and 83rd minutes, Rodney provided them. Sublime goals that sent 7,000 fans at the Vic along with one presenter and four supposedly neutral pundits on the *Soccer Saturday* set into delirium. The impossible was going to happen. Against all the odds, we were staying up. Then in the 89th minute in South Wales, Mark O'Brien chested the ball down and volleyed home a winner for Newport. A defender had scored the goal of his life, saved his club and sent mine tumbling into the National League.

Determined to bounce back at the first attempt, Pools had appointed Craig Harrison, who had done brilliantly at TNS (The New Saints, once Total Network Solutions!) as the new manager. I had met him at a dinner and as well as overseeing a world record breaking twenty-seven consecutive wins at TNS (toppling the previous holders Ajax), he was a really good bloke. He walked a leg of one of my prostate cancer marathons and we discussed winning the first six games of the season and never being caught. In fact, we won none of them.

I didn't realise – and nor did Craig – what a financial mess we were in. The owner John Blackledge took over a club in turmoil on and off the field. There had been winding up orders. The club had turned up for a match at Leyton Orient without training kit or bibs as a local launderette refused to hand them back until bills were paid. Blackledge was leaving others to run the club on a daily basis, it was haemorrhaging his money and he soon pulled the plug.

Harrison had no chance. The club could afford no internet at the training ground, so there was no watching of videos of future opponents. By the end, his wife was coming to the club to cook meals for the players or buy sandwiches for them.

Fast forward to the 2020–21 season. Blackledge had sold the club for £1 to Raj Singh (with a small contribution from me). Debts were cleared, Raj invested more than he had promised and Dave Challinor was the manager. But in three years since relegation from the Football League we had finished fifteenth, fifteenth and twelfth. To be honest, I had given up on ever getting back. The National League was brimful of sides who had played in the EFL – Notts County (founder members of the Football League), Chesterfield, Stockport, Yeovil, Barnet. Wrexham, who once famously beat Arsenal in an FA Cup tie, had been there since 2008.

Shamefully, only one team goes up automatically – Sutton United clinched that spot by beating us. We had topped the table for part of the season but eventually finished fourth, which meant that in the National League's complex but effective play-off system we had to win three one-off games to clinch promotion. We beat Bromley 3–2 in the eliminator round and then against the odds went to Stockport, who were unbeaten in eighteen games, and won through a brilliant goal from Rhys Oates. It meant we would meet league runners-up Torquay in the final at Bristol City's Ashton Gate.

Earlier in the season Hartlepool's home game against Torquay had been televised live on BT Sport. It kicked off at 5.20, so as I didn't come off the air until 5.30 and would be driving home, I had recorded the match. I gave Paul Merson strict instructions not to text me about the game. He could hardly contain himself as we were three down at half-time and lost 5–0! I was blissfully unaware of the outcome as I sat down to watch it when I got back to Winchester.

My son Robbie and I drove to the final on 19 June – a day after England had played Scotland in the European Championships. My wife Lizzie and other son Matt were watching at home. Robbie's housemates at Loughborough University huddled around a TV with his girlfriend Alex. Many of the 3,000 Poolies allowed into the game had made a weekend of it and spent a night on the town the previous evening.

I'm a nervous watcher at the best of times, but I could barely eat or drink before the game. My stomach was churning – and it was a good judge. It turned out to be one of the most dramatic play-off finals of any division.

Pools took the lead after 35 minutes through Luke Armstrong and were unlucky not to be further ahead at half-time. But Torquay, who had already had one goal disallowed, then had another ruled out controversially. We lost the talismanic Oates to injury and Torquay took control. The minutes passed agonisingly slowly as we edged towards the finish line and promotion. Then six minutes of added time. Five had gone when Torquay won a corner. Their giant goalkeeper Lucas Covolan came forward. But our defence managed to clear it. A huge sigh of relief from 3,000 souls.

But wait. The ball was launched back into the Hartlepool box. Covolan was still there. Our young goalkeeper Brad James came to collect but in the throng of players inside the box got nowhere near the ball. Covolan did, his header finding the net. I glanced at the referee and assistant in hope of a reprieve. But there was none. Torquay fans were elated. The Hartlepool contingent deflated. On the pitch, the Hartlepool team collectively sank to its knees. Behind the dugout, our left-back David Ferguson, who had been subbed, exhausted 15 minutes from time, could not hold back the tears. There could surely be only one winner of this game now.

But somehow Dave Challinor regrouped his team and extra-time failed to produce another goal. It would be the dreaded penalty shootout. The manager had chosen his takers and the order – there would be no volunteering. Luke Molineux had come off the bench with 30 seconds remaining. His only kick in the final would be from the spot.

Pools went first, but the ever reliable Nicky Featherstone, our No. 1 penalty taker, saw Covolan spring to his right and save. Despair. But Billy Waters missed for Torquay and suddenly there was hope. But Covolan saved again, this time from Armstrong. It was hard to imagine missing your first two penalties and winning. Incredibly, the veteran Danny Wright missed the second Torquay penalty. It was unwatchable, unbearable stuff as cramp-stricken, exhausted Mark Shelton stepped up for the third Pools penalty. I didn't know at the time that he had never taken a penalty – not even in training. Covalan walked off his line to tell Shelts that he would save it. He didn't and Pools were in front again, but Asa Hall levelled. Jamie Sterry, Molineux with his one touch in the final and Danny Elliott scored the next three for Pools. Each time Torquay responded. Pools skipper Ryan Donaldson put us back in front. But Brad James had yet to get close to saving any

Torquay penalty. Matt Buse stepped up to keep Torquay in it. I can remember what happened next so clearly, almost dreamlike, as if I am reliving it in slow motion. Buse hit his shot hard to the keeper's right. James guessed correctly and flung himself towards it, getting just enough contact to divert it upwards against the crossbar. We had done it.

I hugged the breath out of my son, the manager's wife Kate and her sons, the chairman's sons, the club doctor and his wife, anyone within hugging distance. I couldn't hold back the tears.

My phone was going crazy, the high-pitched pings of messages of congratulations arriving with the speed of machine gun fire.

On the pitch it was mayhem too. After the trophy presentation Robbie and I made a beeline for the celebrating team. I spotted Dave Challinor being led to the BT interview position. I apologised to the floor manager who was with him as I leapt into his arms.

The 3,000 fans sounded like 30,000 as player after player lifted the trophy in front of them. Then the chairman did the same. To be honest I didn't want to steal the players' limelight but Mark Shelton thrust the cup into my hands. Now the crowd was chanting my name. Time for more tears. I wanted it to never end, but an hour or so later we headed off this field of dreams. As we walked back towards the stands, close to the dugout, the Torquay manager Gary Johnson approached

Robbie and I with top man and top manager
David Challinor after Pools' promotion back to the EFL.
Carelessly, within two seasons we had lost him
and our League status.

us, offering his hand and his congratulations. It was the
mark of a truly classy human being. Torquay fans felt
they had been robbed by some bad officiating. Worse
would follow for them with another relegation, to the
National League South, a couple of years later.

Hartlepool's team celebrations went on long into the
night, but we drove home. Lizzie, Matt and my daughter
Olivia were waiting with champagne, gifts and cards.
I had forgotten it was Father's Day. Now it would be a
Father's Day that I would never ever forget.

Ironically, just two years later we had thrown it all away. Bad managerial appointments, bad recruitment, bad performances and bad results meant we were back where we started – in the National League. Not one of the players who stepped forward to take a spot-kick that day was still at the club by then. Still, if we get to another play-off final, hopefully, and with no disrespect to Ashton Gate, it will be at Wembley Stadium!

19

THE DAY THE SKY FELL IN

It was a Wednesday in August 2020 when the sky fell in on *Soccer Saturday*.

I had been driving to a voiceover session for Sky Bet at a small studio in Amble in Hampshire when I had a puncture. I limped (well the car did) into a near-empty business park, took one look at the size of the spare wheel for the Range Rover and took the only sensible course of action – I rang the AA. It turned out to be the only good phone call all day.

It was a lovely, sunny mid-morning and I was wondering how to spend the next hour or so until the yellow van containing the automobile cavalry arrived, blissfully unaware of the storm clouds gathering. I need not have worried about killing time. Almost immediately, my phone rang. It was Phil Thompson. He told me that he had been told that Gary Hughes, the head of football at Sky, wanted to speak to him via Zoom at 11 and wondered if I had any idea of what it might be about. Though we are the best of friends, Phil would rarely ring out of the blue. He was obviously concerned. Thommo had already spoken to Charlie Nicholas in Glasgow who had been asked to speak to Gary at midday.

We mulled over the possibilities. The boys had done a lot of work remotely during the pandemic and we were hoping that we would all soon be re-united in the studio. We wondered if the call would be to tell them that was the case or possibly that they would still be in the Wilmslow and Glasgow studios.

Could it be a pay rise? Or a pay cut? Both Thommo and Charlie had a little while left on their contracts so that seemed unlikely.

Inwardly though, I was panicking a little. In recent years, I'd had to fight for Thommo's place on the panel. Two years previously I'd had a meeting with Gary and fellow Sky executive Steve Smith. I was told that the panel needed to change and that Thommo would be sacrificed. After all, younger fans might not know him. After much debate they were unmoved. But as a last resort, I suggested *Soccer Saturday* kept all four – Phil, Charlie, Matt Le Tissier and Merse – but rotated them so that three would work every week and newcomers could be integrated into the team. We had done something similar in the early years of the show when George Best, Rodney Marsh and Frank McLintock had been supplemented by the likes of Alan Mullery, Nigel Spackman, Peter Reid and David Ginola.

To my relief Gary and Steve agreed. It would not be quite the same, but not far off. Every Saturday one of our gang got to enjoy a weekend off while Clinton Morrison, Tim Sherwood, Joleon Lescott or Glen Johnson came in to learn the art of shouting wildly and loudly every time the ball came within 25 yards of the goal.

When Rob Webster was appointed as managing director of Sky Sports in May 2019, I asked for a meeting and raised the subject of Thommo's status. I told him that in my opinion the argument that younger fans could not relate to him was nonsense, that any proper football fan would remember him. And even if some younger viewers didn't remember his on-field triumphs, they would certainly know him as a top football pundit. Rob's response was not encouraging. He told me his teenage sons would probably relate more to a recently retired thirty-two-year-old ex-Norwich City player than they would to Phil.

'Ok,' I said. 'You find me a recently retired thirty-two-year old who has won seven league titles, three European Cups, captained his country and club, who can talk intelligently, eloquently and passionately on any footballing topic and who is willing to spend six hours every Saturday afternoon and I will have no problem with that person replacing Thommo.'

The MD took a neutral stance – at least at that stage, perhaps because I was in full flow. He had not come from a production background and reckoned he could not make decisions about who was or was not on the panel. I had hoped he might think I was in a position to make that sort of call or take my advice, but I was wrong.

Moments after I put the phone down to Thommo, I knew what the fate of my mates was going to be. My mobile buzzed again. It was Matt Le Tissier.

'Hi mate, how are you?' I asked.

'Well, I was ok until five minutes ago when Sky fucking sacked me,' he said.

Now Tiss had been extremely controversial on social media, particularly, but not exclusively, over Covid and there had been times on the show when I felt I was sitting next to the new David Icke. But I don't have to share his views to get on well with him. His forthrightness made him a compelling panel member, he has a great sense of humour (he drinks Malibu and Coke for goodness sake) and was a genius of a footballer. In Southampton, they used to think he walked to Guernsey when he went home. Of course he was also a little more contemporary than Thommo and Charlie. If he was getting the bullet, so were they.

I rang Thommo back and let him know the news. All we could do was to wait for the inevitable. As the minutes dragged past, the AA man replaced the tyre. But I was deflated and there was nothing he could do for me. By 12 both had texted me one-word messages. 'Sacked.' This felt like an out-of-body experience. How could they be dismantling a team that had been standard bearers at Sky for so long? How could they do it without even talking to me about it?

At around 12.15 my mobile buzzed again. It was Gary Hughes, the head of football. Suddenly it dawned on me that this could be the call telling me I was finished too. No one is indispensable and though over the years he and I had got on well, in recent years there had been disagreements. And I am sometimes too opinionated for my own good – a little dogmatic to be honest – or a little gobshite, depending on your point of view. I had been too worried about the boys' fate and had not considered mine.

But I was safe and so was Paul Merson.

Hughes explained that he and Steve Smith had decided it was the right time for change. 'How can it be the right time?' I blurted out. 'The season gets underway in a couple of weeks and you have sacked three of our team. It's like Man City selling De Bruyne, Gundogan and Silva two weeks before kick-off, their entire midfield, their engine room. And we have no one to replace them with.'

Gary insisted it *was* the right time and that they had people who could step into the biggest of broadcasting shoes and proceeded to reel off a list of people.

After each name I made a quickfire judgement. 'No good.' 'Terminally dull.' 'Doesn't even like football.' 'Oh, for fuck's sake.' That gives you the general tone. I was devastated and as Gary listed the names of potential replacements, I knew I had a decision to make too about my future.

Matt Roberts, the *Soccer Saturday* producer, rang. He had just been told of the blood-letting and was equally shocked. He was the man who had to rebuild the team – and quickly. Even Sir Alex would have struggled.

Merse was next on, wondering how he had escaped the cull and whether he should resign.

'Merse,' I said, 'you have fifteen kids and no money. Of course you should not resign. Whatever you do mate, keep on taking the money. The boys wouldn't want you to resign and whatever I end up doing you have to continue. Anyway, it's all down to you from now on mate to carry that show.' I was exaggerating about the number of kids, but not the money!

I had to turn off the phone while I recorded 'Sky Bet, that's Betting Better' in fifty different ways. By the time I switched it back on, the world had gone mad. I had literally hundreds of messages and missed calls, all wanting to know if the rumours they had heard were really true.

Twitter was alive with the sackings. Some people felt my silence meant I must be complicit, which confirms everyone is entitled to an opinion, even if you are hopelessly, embarrassingly wide of the mark.

I took my time to think about things, assess if there was any chance of Sky having a change of heart, pondered potential new panellists and whether I would ever look at them in the same light as my mates.

A week or so before the opening game of the new season, I had come to a decision. It was one of the toughest decisions I'd ever had to make. But I had talked about it with my family. Many tears had been shed but I knew the course of action I had to take. I would have to give up the job I loved. With a heavy heart, I e-mailed Rob Webster, the MD, and told him that neither I nor the majority of viewers could ever agree with or accept the decision to sack Thommo, Tiss and Charlie. As the company was clearly cost-cutting, I asked that they pay me up. 'After twenty-eight years I am sad to have to ask this,' I concluded.

Webster asked to speak to me. I had gone to the family bolt hole just outside Olhos de Agua in Portugal to get away from it all for a few days. I often used it as a refuge when I needed time. We agreed to speak on the Sunday morning. It was a glorious sunny Algarvian day in contrast to my dark mood. It was a long, difficult conversation. I always found Rob easy to talk with but more difficult to coax actions from. I suspect he was not having an easy time in his job either. But finally he asked if I would give it a try for one more season and, if at the end of that season, I was still unhappy I could leave and he would guarantee me a good deal. I told him that, hand on heart, I did not know whether I would be able to finish the season but I was at least willing to start it. I didn't feel any joy in agreeing to stay, more shame that I should have gone with the boys. But Thommo, Charlie and Tiss were never critical of my decision and my regard . . . no, my respect . . . oh bugger it, my love for them only increased!

And so on 12 September that season, *Soccer Saturday* and I returned. Arsenal won at Fulham, Liverpool beat Leeds 4–3 and Hartlepool avoided defeat (their season didn't start until October!). Social media was awash with criticism of the new line-up. Hand on heart, I cannot remember who was on the panel that day. I only knew it was not the people I wanted alongside me.

Two days later Rob Webster e-mailed me. 'Great to have the new season up and running.'

20

RESIGNING (AGAIN)

On 5 August 2021, two days before a new EFL season was due to kick-off, I resigned again. Different reasons, different managing director, but this was becoming a very bad habit.

Having committed myself to another season at Sky, I was soon regretting it. Rather than being seen as someone willing to help the company through a difficult time (of their own making), I felt like a troublesome schoolboy, made to sit at the front of class and never allowed to speak.

Just before the 2020–2021 season got underway, I had given an interview to Don McRae at the *Guardian*, ostensibly about my new book *I've Got Mail*. It had been arranged by the publishers long before the sackings and I honoured the agreement. I hadn't asked permission from Sky because in more than twenty years, I hadn't asked permission to be interviewed and no one had ever complained.

Don wrote a lovely, sympathetic piece in which I gave my views on many things – the emergence of women in football and broadcasting, how I had unwittingly helped save someone's life (a story for another book) and of course the sackings of Thommo, Charlie and Tiss. I admitted I had thought about quitting, which was common knowledge. But I dodged questions like 'Did Sky just decide there were too many old white men on *Soccer Saturday*?' by the straight bat response of 'I am not privy to their decisions'. And I tried to stress the positives, concluding, 'It is the start of a new journey, let's see where it takes us'.

I loved it. My bosses hated it.

I was told Sky needed advance notice and articles like this had to be signed off by the internal communications team. I was barred from doing an interview on 5 Live the following day and told my publishers there would be no more promotional interviews.

Despite the lack of publicity, *I've Got Mail* did well enough to be shortlisted in the *Daily Telegraph's* Sports Book Awards that year.

But the bigger problems were both on screen and behind the scenes. With Covid still rife, it would have been difficult regardless of the changes to the show. Sky was trying hard to return to some form of normality – and during the pandemic, the company had been wonderfully supportive of staff. But people were still encouraged to come to the office only when essential, one-way systems prevailed, testing was required. Drinks parties and get-togethers of any sort were of course banned. The glue-like bond that had made us such a tight team was coming unstuck. Going to work was now like, well going to work. For years it had been fun. I was lucky enough to be in a job that I loved going to, working with people that I loved working with. As with life in general at that time, things were just not the same

And every single person knew that it had been a mistake to sack the boys.

Covid had a huge impact on the show that year as well. Premier League matches were all being shown live as games were still behind closed doors. So Saturday's games were EFL. Our shows were shortened – not ideal for a new team of pundits trying to develop a rapport. Worse, due to social distancing rules, I would have only Merse and one other alongside me, with two others in a separate studio, and one left to his own devices in a third studio. No Premier League, short shows, a new panel, socially distanced – it was the perfect storm.

I believe the first new panel was Merse, Clinton Morrison, Tim Sherwood, Glen Johnson and Tony Pulis. I would taunt Thommo by telling him we had replaced him with someone younger and more popular – Tony Pulis! It was often tough going but I knew that if a goalkeeper made a mistake trying to play out from the back I could go to Tony, who would always have steam coming out of his ears at such tippy-tappy nonsense. Tony, who is a smashing guy, quickly learned the name of the game. He knew I would come to him immediately Ederson or Alisson or De Gea had been caught out. And he always delivered the required rant.

When I bumped into people, the first thing they would say was no longer 'Unbelievable Jeff' but 'It's not the same'. I would always toe the party line by replying that people had thought George Best, Rodney Marsh and Frank McLintock were irreplaceable but it takes time for people to accept change. We were also constantly changing the line-up to include Joleon Lescott, Sue Smith, Ally McCoist, Kris Boyd and even Neil Warnock on one occasion (he was brilliant by the way). There were a host of others too as we scrambled to find the right formula.

Sometimes though our newcomers did not help themselves. One week I was about to launch into a section of the show which would discuss a handful of hugely controversial refereeing and VAR decisions from Premier League games played in midweek. One of our panel asked me not to involve him as he had not seen any of the midweek matches. Don't get me wrong – I don't expect our pundits to watch every minute of every game but in this day and age it is so simple to catch up online. I liked this person a great deal, but this to me was unforgivable. On another occasion, during the game he was covering, Fulham brought on a substitute. Our expert had not heard of him before and did not know where he played. It was Fulham's No. 10, Tom Cairney. He had played more than 280 games for the club!

I was concerned too that all our sparky, humorous features – the two-team league in the Scilly Isles who played each other every week, but still conducted a draw for their cup competition; the worst side in the UK (it wasn't yours unless you are a fan of football in the Isle of Arran); the footballer turned wrestler (Grant Holt); goalkeeper Richard Lee and his headwear business Dr Cap and so on – had completely been halted while some of my favourite match reporters, the likes of Ian Dowie and Tony Cottee, were being phased out to be replaced by every Tom, Dick and Harriet, or so it seemed.

But we lurched on. From time to time I was told how viewing figures were actually up on the previous season as if this was some sort of guide to how well the show was doing. The fact that no fans were allowed to attend matches and that we were showing goals as they went in from EFL games made it pretty obvious that figures would be good.

During this time I was being consulted over virtually nothing. I had no input into panel line-ups or reporters. When we needed a new producer as Matt Roberts moved on, I was told who it would be, rather than being asked who I thought might be a good fit. When I did suggest a name, it was dismissed without consideration. I was being increasingly marginalised. I was becoming increasingly concerned about the future – and my future at Sky. In March, those concerns multiplied after a series of exchanges with the MD Rob Webster and I became convinced that rather than me wanting to leave, the company wanted me out.

Firstly Webster contacted me to ask if I wanted to carry on with the show the following season. He told me the company needed to know as it was the end of their financial year and they were working on bonuses for the following year and needed to know if they had to factor me in. It frankly made no sense to me.

In a subsequent phone call, I asked him if there was

a doubt in his mind over whether I would be presenting *Soccer Saturday* the following season. He told me he would take the Fifth Amendment on that – hardly re-assuring. When I pressed him he told me some people doubted my enthusiasm and commitment to the show. I exploded, 'Just tell them to turn on their TV at 12 this Saturday. They'll see how much fucking enthusiasm and commitment I've got!'

Within a couple of weeks of the conversation, Rob Webster had left the company.

But I had many doubts about the company's long-term belief in me and asked for a meeting with the new MD Jonathan Licht. We had spoken briefly at a couple of functions previously but didn't really know each other. At our first meeting I dropped the bombshell that I wanted to leave. I had pressures at home, my daughter was unwell and I was finding it too hard to be the smiling face of *Soccer Saturday*.

Jonathan was dumbstruck. I found him an incredibly nice, warm human being. Considerate and easy to talk to – which was just as well as a few months later I would need his influence to help me stay at Sky. He understood my issues and why I wanted to go. The first thing he needed to know though was that I would be presenting when the new season kicked off in just 48 hours' time. Of course, I re-assured him, I would. In the end, with a mid-season change likely to put the company in a tricky position, I agreed to stay until the end of the season on condition I just did Saturdays and no midweek *Soccer Specials*.

One Saturday several weeks later, the entire production team and the pundits due to appear that afternoon were told that there would be an announcement at 10.30 by the head of football, Gary Hughes. We crowded into a conference room. Reporters – among them Bianca Westwood – and others joined via Zoom. Gary made the announcement. I felt relief that finally I could tell the truth to people who I had deceived while the details of my departure were finalised. My phone started to ping. The first message came from Bianca. She said simply, 'You bastard!'

That afternoon we announced the news on *Soccer Saturday*. Sky Sports News ran the story. The national media all covered it. There was no turning back. Except there was!

The future was looking bright. I accepted an offer from 5 Live to present a Sunday morning radio show. I had lunches with talkSPORT over the possibility of resurrecting a results show with the old gang of Thommo, Le Tiss, Charlie and Merse on Talk TV. I had lunch at the Ivy in Richmond with Amanda Holden to discuss co-hosting a game show. I had agreed a podcast alongside Kammy.

But my anorexic teenage daughter's health was deteriorating rapidly. In March, Olivia was admitted to hospital in London. I genuinely thought she would not come out alive. Every single day, week after week, my wife Lizzie and I would make a near six-hour round trip to visit her. On Friday evenings, I would be at the hospital until 8.30 p.m., then stay overnight at the Novotel in Brentford. After the show the following day, I would head straight back to the hospital. My wife and I were physically and mentally shattered.

A handful of people in my office knew what was happening. I needed to talk about what my family was going through. Carly Bassett and Marianne Bremner who sat next to me would listen, comfort and provide a shoulder to cry on. As did producer Sam Mills and Jonathan Licht. Sometimes I would be in tears in my dressing room minutes before going on air, wondering if my beautiful girl would ever get well.

We had been to visit Olivia one Sunday when I knew what I had to do. I could not be dashing off to Manchester for the BBC or racing around the country for podcasts. I didn't want to host a game show where I was meant to make people laugh and smile. I needed to be as close to my daughter as I could be and I need to be surrounded by my friends and family. Lizzie and my boys Robbie and Matt agreed.

On Monday morning I e-mailed the head of football. 'This is not the e-mail you might have been expecting this morning.' I asked for my job back – if it wasn't too late. Later that day I drove to Sky HQ in Isleworth to meet with Jonathan, Gary Hughes and Steve Smith. They listened sympathetically. They needed to be pragmatic though. It was no use them letting me stay on if three months later I changed my mind. Would I guarantee staying for at least one more year? I would.

Jonathan Licht stayed up into the early hours of the night to get confirmation from Sky owners, Comcast, that they could tear up my resignation and termination agreement. On Thursday of that week at 2.45 p.m. I e-mailed the BBC, the podcast providers, my agent, my publisher and anyone else I could think of who had been expecting me to work for them in the future. At 3.00 Sky Sports News' lead story was 'We reveal Jeff Stelling's replacement. It is . . . Jeff Stelling.' Gary Hughes told me later that Sky had originally intended to offer the *Soccer Saturday* role to someone on that Tuesday. My e-mail had arrived just 24 hours beforehand. I had saved my job in the equivalent of Fergie Time.

21

END GAME

There was a price to pay for my return, quite literally. I was asked to take a pay cut. This wasn't unreasonable as I had asked to be excused from any midweek shows. Ironically, on 'The Pundits' tour with Charlie, Phil, Matt and Merse, people frequently remarked that I must have changed my mind because I had been offered a salary hike. Nothing could have been further from the truth.

But I also had to accept some alterations to the show format. Instead of discussing each of the weekend's games, we would spend the first hour or more debating the main issues of the week. This was a nod to *The Debate* which had been a late night Sky Sports show a number of years previously and which I had presented from time to time. I loved this new opening element of *Soccer Saturday* because it could produce some feisty arguments. The topics could also change on the morning of the show if there had been an overnight sacking or signing so it could be a challenge, but I felt it was a very positive change. The segments featuring Fantasy Premier League and the EFL or Scotland worked less well. I think the Fantasy Premier League section was part of the continuing attempt to attract younger viewers. The truth is no one of any age could be interested in our Fantasy Football picks. Merse was so disinterested he still had Joao Cancelo in his team months after his loan from Manchester City to Bayern Munich.

The attempt to entice younger viewers is flawed in my opinion. Firstly, in general they don't pay the bills! And secondly, they have so many alternative ways of accessing the things they want to see. I believe TV should be focused on making quality programming to hold on to the current audience. By the time those missing younger viewers get to be mid-thirties or parents, they will hopefully be attracted to regular TV programming by that quality. But Sky, like many, believe their future is with younger viewers. At the start of the 2023–24 Premier League season, they trumpeted that over 8 million viewers had watched the opening weekend, including 2.5 million under-thirty-fives. Age may be just a number, but it is a critical one in the eyes of Sky.

The EFL section lacked imagination and those fun features that I have already banged on about earlier. It only came to life when Neil Warnock took over at Huddersfield!

We introduced a segment live from one of the games of the day usually hosted by Katie Shanahan, Jaydee Dyer or Emma Saunders alongside an ex-player. In general this worked well, but sometimes the choice of guest had me scratching my head. For instance, near the end of the season we were live from Villa Park. Courtney Sweetman-Kirk, the ex-Sheffield United women's striker was the pundit. Alan McInally, the former Aston Villa striker, who had scored in a European Cup semi-final for Bayern Munich, texted me.

'While Courtney is at Villa Park, I am at home cutting the fucking lawn!' This was no slight on Courtney, but the big man was a blindingly obvious choice to be the pre-match pundit.

Approaching kick-off, reporters delivered team news from the grounds in the top two divisions along with a handful of games in the lower EFL divisions and Scotland. But these were recorded 45 minutes before kick-off when the stadia were deserted. Not a good look! And away from the Premier League I wondered about the value of team news anyway. Outside of Rotherham, was anyone really aware of what impact Tyler Blackett would have coming into the team against Bristol City while Shane Ferguson dropped to the bench? No, I thought not. In fact, the answer was not a great deal as he was subbed at half-time.

But my daughter was home from hospital and I was among friends, so I simply got on with it.

Away from Sky, 'The Pundits' tour was going well. We travelled the UK from Southampton to Aberdeen, Cardiff to Southend. We performed the same show at La Manga in Spain. The only really dark cloud on the horizon was Matt Le Tissier's controversial comments on social media – though Tiss would probably have told you it wasn't a dark cloud, it was a fake! But Le Tiss was in his element on the golf course. The event could not have gone better. The eventual winner's prize was given to the team that finished second, with the real winners getting nothing. Tiss thought it was a conspiracy. I thought it was a cock-up.

•

Back at Sky, cracks were beginning to appear. I will admit in terms of work, I am demanding. I'm not a perfectionist because I know everyone makes mistakes. But I want everything to be done as well as humanly possible. I didn't think that was always the case in my final season at *Soccer Saturday*.

We carried an interview with Newcastle United's goalkeeper Nick Pope. It was really interesting, partly because we rarely heard from him. As everyone will tell you I am a big fan of Pope and rate him in the top ten in the world. That brought about an argument worthy of any debate. But the following week, the running order contained an interview with . . . Nick Pope. I thought it was a mistake but when I queried it, I was told that it had been done by *Soccer AM* and was different to the previous week. So not having heard from Pope all season, we would hear from him twice in two weeks. The smoke was rising from my ears and eventually the second interview was dropped.

Similarly we ran an interview with Aston Villa striker Ollie Watkins when the week before we had carried a piece with the same player. It was over six minutes long, an eternity in TV terms. When I complained about it all, I was told by the producer it would give us all a nice break. I didn't want a nice break, thank you. I wanted a piece that would leave viewers glued to their set.

Another week we were scheduled to run a piece with Liverpool manager Jurgen Klopp. Klopp was being a brilliant sport by taking part in some physicality challenges using tackle dummies with reporter Joe Tomlinson. Again this had originally been shot for another show and I was unhappy about using it. At this stage, Liverpool were struggling badly by their standards in the Premier League. That week Klopp had given a Champions League press conference on Monday, overseen the game on Tuesday, had received the Freedom of the City of Liverpool on Wednesday and done pre-match media duties on Friday before a game at the weekend. Yet he had still found time to shoot the feature with Joe. Or I thought he had. I suggested mischievously that while we were delighted that he had given up his time, some Liverpool fans might be thinking he was spending too much of his energies on non-team matters. I was shot down in flames by the panel, but the Liverpool press office reacted immediately by threatening that Klopp would not speak to Sky on the following afternoon's *Super Sunday*. Gary Hughes was on the phone to producer Sam Mills. I waited for the bollocking. None came. Then I was informed that they had failed to tell me that the interview hadn't actually been done during Klopp's busy week, but around three weeks before. No one had told me it was an old interview. I had been hung out to dry. But I still had to make an on-air apology.

I was also getting concerned about what I was hearing about the future. The following season there would be a new studio designed for a presenter plus five guests. I had always railed against having five pundits. It was busy enough with four and a constant battle to ensure everyone got relatively equal amounts of airtime. Rather like a schoolteacher struggling with class size, this would be too unwieldy, I believed. In the end it turned out to be a presenter plus six. The new studio would be automated. Was I being replaced by AI? I wasn't sure. And it would be paperless. I handwrite all my stats. I want to know at a glance that Crystal Palace's Will Hughes had scored for the first time in fifty-eight league games. Or that James Milner was making his 332nd appearance for Liverpool when he came on at Southampton, as well as becoming their oldest ever Premier League player, eclipsing Gary McAllister. You need to get the stats out instantly, not minutes later. I was told I would have an iPad.

Just a minute dear viewers while I access the Crystal Palace website and count up the number of games since Will Hughes scored . . . It couldn't work – or at least not for me.

No one mentioned that ref Mike Dean would also be incorporated into the panel – they must have feared I would give that the red card too. I have no problems with Mike – I thought he was one of our very best referees. But one of the most engaging parts of the show was arguing over debatable decisions. Having an expert in the studio would kill that straightaway. And I was not sure having Mike covering a game would be welcomed by fans any more than when on the odd occasion we used reality TV stars to watch matches during midweek *Soccer Specials*. The one occasion I did feel using a celebrity worked was when comedian Tom Allen went to Charlton with Mark McAdam as a match reporter. Tom knew absolutely nothing about football and is no Alan McInally. But his contributions were hilarious – at least for a while. We could have done without the game finishing 5–2 to be honest as you can have too much of a good thing. But it was a brilliant one-off idea and the public reaction was rightly favourable.

I also learned that our long-serving PA, Marianne McCarthy, would not be working on the show the following season. For years she had been my right-hand man, sorry woman, sorry person. We would plan the timing of the show together – how much was needed on each item. She would count me in and out of breaks and VTs during the show, she would let me know how long we had used in any discussion and how long we had remaining, she would shuffle the running order during a programme when I asked her, she would ensure I said my 'Goodnight' to the second as well as a million other things. If I toppled off the broadcasting cliff edge, she was holding the safety net.

When I complained about the changes I was told 'That's progress'. Viewers will be the best judges of whether they felt the show had progressed by the following season.

I still adored the programme – as it built to a crescendo each week it was impossible not to get a buzz from it – but increasingly I felt I was swimming against a rip tide. The effort of getting through Saturday was taking a toll. I still feel ashamed to admit this as I remembered my dad looking grey, grimy and thoroughly knackered after working a shift at the steelworks in Hartlepool. But I would not only be shattered after each show but was also feeling a constant tightness in my chest, presumably caused by the stress.

I knew what I had to do, a feeling strengthened when I heard that all Sky's football reporters had been told they would have to reapply for their jobs. Among them was Geoff Shreeves. In the early days we did not always see eye-to-eye but during my stint on the Champions League, we got to know each other better and our relationship improved. One thing was never in doubt – he has long been the best tunnel reporter in the business. It is one of the trickiest of all jobs and not one I would like to do. Close friends of mine Bianca Westwood, Dickie Davis, Johnny Phillips, Greg Whelan and Jaydee Dyer, considered a rising star at Sky, were others who faced interviews to keep their jobs. Most knew their fate long before the decisions. Johnny was the only one to survive the cull.

I met Jonathan Licht and Gary Hughes to complete the hat-trick of resignations. I told them how the show was affecting me and what I felt the issues were. Jonathan, understanding as ever, offered me the rest of the season off so I could come back in August refreshed and well. But this time I knew I was three and out. Sky would be generous in my departure terms.

But thereafter it was, as Merse would say, like a scene from *Platoon* as big name after big name fell on the broadcasting battlefield.

As well as my reporter friends, my long-time pal Graeme Souness departed. Souey was a wonderful throwback to the times when players spent 90 minutes kicking each other, hugged at the final whistle and had a beer together afterwards. In TV terms he often spoke for the older generation, my generation, who preferred their football without the diving, the feigning of injury, the time-wasting. I don't think Sky had ever truly forgiven him for the day at Chelsea that he called football 'a man's game'. It did not help that former England women's star Karen Carney was sitting alongside him. It was just a piece of terminology that had been used since the dawn of person-kind and he meant no insult by it, but such are the verbal traps that face every broadcaster these days. It spoke volumes of the man that soon after leaving, at the age of seventy, he swam the Channel to raise funds in the fight against epidermolysis bullosa after being moved by the plight of fourteen-year-old Isla Grist.

Next out of the building was Martin Tyler, the man simply known as 'The Voice' during his decades at Sky. We had worked together on and off since the 1984 Olympics. He rang me soon after the decision. There was no bitterness. We both knew we had enjoyed wonderful times at Sky. But we both knew there was still some broadcasting life in us yet. Beyond question, Tyler is up there with the Wolstenholmes, Motsons and Davies of football commentary.

Soccer AM, a Saturday morning staple for almost thirty years, was scrapped seemingly with little thought as to what would replace it. Changing attitudes had been challenging for the show – ladettes had long since become unacceptable. But in its latest re-incarnation, figures had been decent and in John Fendley's hands – Fenners to you and me – it seemed to be enjoying a renaissance. Eventually *Saturday Social* would be extended into its slot, a show that relies on YouTubers' likes and dislikes with none of the life or fun of *Soccer AM*. The eternal quest for yoof continues, so sadly misguided.

My big pal Alan McInally, a man who brought authority, passion, energy and, in his view, suaveness to proceedings, was told his contract would not be renewed after the final game of the season and he would be given matches to cover on an ad-hoc basis. Instead, the likes of former England fast bowler Stuart Broad appeared on the panel for mid-week *Soccer Specials*. Stuart is a big Nottingham Forest fan but what sort of footballing insight would he bring to the table? Paul Merson loves his cricket, but would Sky's cricket department ever consider using him? Of course not and rightly so! I mischievously texted an old friend at Sky to suggest that perhaps we should have a panel made up entirely of ex-cricketers! Actually, I would not have minded seeing the brilliant David 'Bumble' Lloyd on the panel, but of course Sky, in their wisdom, got rid of him too.

Julian Warren was apparently told by telephone that he would not be replacing me on *Soccer Saturday*. He had been presenting *Soccer Specials* and standing in for me on Saturdays for ten years. He is a consummate broadcaster. Prepared, eloquent, informed and liked by everyone at *Soccer Saturday*. His experience would have been invaluable in those early chaotic weeks of a new season, which at times was – and I take no pleasure in saying this – car crash television. Possibly the nadir came when we heard a 20 second description of West Ham winning their opening day fixture at Bournemouth, when the pictures and score caption on screen told a different story. The blame for that by the way does not lie just with the presenter. Julian was told apparently that he had not interviewed well enough! The powers that be knew I felt he was the right man for the job, but as was becoming the norm, that counted for nothing. My eventual replacement, Simon Thomas, is a friend and more importantly a very good broadcaster who deserves some breaks after the terrible personal tragedy he suffered with the death of his wife. I just felt Julian had done his time and I did not understand why he was being overlooked. He still performs superbly on midweek *Soccer Specials*.

•

My last day at Sky was Sunday 28 May 2023. I had already agreed to a thirty-date theatre tour of the UK, which would later be extended to forty-two. I was in talks with 5 Live, talkSPORT, Amazon Prime and a major podcast company, Folding Pocket. I had been asked if I would be willing to meet the *Strictly Come Dancing* team. I had done a bit of ballroom dancing as a teenager but only because it was a great place to meet girls. I could not see myself on the show to be honest. Pot-bellied, short-arsed and sequined! I remember Paul Daniels filling the veteran slot one year and he was less than magic, being the first to be booted off the dance floor. It sounded less than appealing (for me that is, god knows how traumatised the audience would have been) so I declined.

I had also been approached by a new reality show with a working title of *Mission to Mars*. I can imagine quite a number of football fans would be more than happy for me to be sent there, but in fact the series would be filmed in the Australian outback (haven't I heard something similar on another reality show?). The producers hoped to recreate the sort of conditions you would find on the Red Planet. I chatted to them via Zoom, appropriately enough, where they told me a lot of big names had been signed up for an American version. But their questions were from another planet. 'What interest do I have in Mars?', 'What is my interest in astronomy?', 'Do I follow the space programme?' None, none and no were my answers. It was as if I was being auditioned for a genuine trip to Mars rather than a game show. I worried this may turn out to be as big a flop as SpaceX's Starship which flew for twenty-four miles when it was launched in the spring of 2023, before it experienced a 'rapid unscheduled disassembly'. Needless to say I was not their Rocket Man and never heard from them again!

A few weeks later ITV offered me an obscene amount of money to appear on their prime-time hit show *The Masked*

Singer. After a lot of thought I turned the offer down. The show has had some bad singers over the years, including Teddy Sheringham and Michael Owen, but my voice would have taken it to a whole new level. Viewers would have turned off in droves, dogs would have howled and cats would have covered their ears. I have the worst voice ever. Equally as important I was due to host events in Ipswich, Plymouth, Newcastle and London and could not make their recording dates work. In the miraculous event of my reaching the final, I would have been The Invisible Singer as I had an event elsewhere. All this is just as well as no doubt someone would have uncovered my tweets from 2020 when the show first appeared. 'Is *The Masked Singer* the worst thing ever to appear on our Saturday night TV?' I asked. 'Take it off, take it off,' and followed that up with 'Oh my gosh, just seen the promo. The bloody *Masked Singer* is on tomorrow night too. Going to go to church instead. Take it off, take it off,' I raged.

During my final week, I got a call at home from Sir Elton John. Danny Baker had told me that Elton watched the show but I had never spoken to him. He could not hear me when I first picked up the phone, but rang back. Elton John rang me back! He was in Paris after just finishing two nights in Barcelona on a European tour. He told me that over years of watching, time and again I had told him Watford were losing, swiftly followed by me announcing Hartlepool were losing. He felt we were kindred spirits. I had been a fan since 1970 and Elton's brilliant second album with 'Take

Me to the Pilot' and 'Border Song'. When I left my sport and music show at Radio Tees to head for London, I played 'Someone Saved My Life Tonight' as my final record. For me this was better than a call from King Charles (sorry Your Royal Majesty!)

I had worked on my final day permutations, something I may not have to do again in the future. For me I had to get it right that day of all days. In truth it was very straight-forward. Abdoulaye Doucoure's goal for Everton against Bournemouth meant it didn't matter what happened to Leeds United and Leicester City – they were both relegated. At the other end, if Aston Villa beat Brighton they would have European football for the first time since 2010. They made my life easy by going two-up inside the first half hour.

Russ Taylor, an outstanding assistant producer and good friend, had without my knowledge put together a lovely tribute piece to effectively close the show. Mates that I hadn't seen for years like Alan Mullery, Frank McLintock, Tony Cottee and Clive Allen sent their best wishes.

My phone was buzzing non-stop. Neil Warnock told me I had retired almost as many times as him. I told him I thought he had at least one more retirement in him – and days later he confirmed he would be staying on as Huddersfield Town manager.

Gordon Strachan, Alan Smith, Kammy, Franny Benali and Jimmy Glass – who helped start it all – messaged. So too old broadcasting mates Max Rushden, Natalie Sawyer, the wonderful Dave Clarke, Hayley McQueen, rugby league legend Eddie Hemmings and Dominic Cork from the cricketing world.

Social media went crazy. Tweets from Gary Lineker, Alastair Campbell, Andy Burnham and dozens of other celebrities. Messages from thousands of people that I have never met, yet who feel like friends, as well as from my wife Lizzie, son Matt and daughter Olivia.

I walked to the third floor of the gloomy, three-quarters empty, multistorey car park, suit carrier over shoulder, briefcase in hand when my phone pinged again. It was a tweet from my son, Robbie.

'Well done, Dad,' it read. 'So proud of you. You have put your heart and soul into the show and have no doubt left a mark on more than just the world of football. As a father and broadcaster, you have taught me so much about football and life. You are the best there has ever been x.'

I climbed into my car and drove away from Sky on the all too familiar route towards my home, my family and a new journey ahead.

EPILOGUE

In the time since I have left Sky I still hear the cries of 'Unbelievable Jeff!' from passers-by and black-cab drivers. But often it is now accompanied with 'It isn't the same anymore, Jeff'. That saddens me as that was never my intention when I left *Soccer Saturday*.

I won't lie. I no longer watch the show that was my life for almost three decades. Not because I feel any ill-will. Just the opposite. I have many friends working on the programme and I am desperate for it to succeed. But if I watched, I know that as an opinionated little so-and-so I would sit and criticise which would benefit no one. Instead, I would rather celebrate nearly thirty years of doing the best job in the world.

I am lucky that so many people believe there is life in this old dog yet and have offered me projects. Not many people are still learning about and enjoying new roles at my age.

My radio show at talkSPORT has been a joy. In my first couple of weeks, under cajoling from my Breakfast partner Ally McCoist, I revealed I did not like gravy on my

Christmas turkey. The message boards lit up more than ever over 'Gravygate'. It felt a little over the top when someone suggested it was the first sign that I was on my way to becoming a serial killer. Even if people were not seeing me anymore, they were still listening and reacting. It has been different gravy.

People also shout 'Enjoy your retirement, Jeff!' And I am sure I will. Just not yet . . .

Acknowledgements

With thanks to:

The late Vic Wakeling who entrusted me with *Soccer Saturday* then encouraged and supported me.

Charlie, Thommo, Merse, Tiss and Kammy for providing me with so much material.

Bianca Westwood for laughing at the same punchlines every night during the 'Me and Bee' tour.

Everyone at talkSPORT for allowing me the chance to show there is life after sixty-eight.

Jonathan Taylor and the team at Headline, as well as Tom Whiting.

Football fans, male and female, throughout the nation and beyond. Whichever colours you wear, you have supported me unwaveringly, allowing me to have the career and life that I have described in these pages. Without you, none of this could ever have happened.

PHOTO CREDITS

All photos courtesy of the author except for:

Page 129: courtesy of Jeremy Banks (with thanks to Dianne Stradling at Prostate Cancer UK)

Page 133: courtesy of Sarah Lines (with thanks to Dianne Stradling at Prostate Cancer UK)

Pages 219 and 224: courtesy of Michael Hall McPherson at MHM Media Group